Bret Harte

A Millionaire of Rough-and-Ready and Devil's Ford

Bret Harte

A Millionaire of Rough-and-Ready and Devil's Ford

ISBN/EAN: 9783744652209

Printed in Europe, USA, Canada, Australia, Japan

Cover: Foto ©ninafisch / pixelio.de

More available books at **www.hansebooks.com**

By the same Author.

POEMS. *Cabinet Edition.* 18mo, $1.00.
Household Edition. With Portrait. 12mo, $1.75; gilt, $2.25.
Red-Line Edition. Illustrated. Small 4to, $2.50.
EAST AND WEST POEMS. 16mo, $1.50.
THE LUCK OF ROARING CAMP, etc. 16mo, $1.50.
MRS. SKAGGS'S HUSBANDS, etc. 16mo, $1.50.
TALES OF THE ARGONAUTS. 16mo, $1.50.
THANKFUL BLOSSOM. 18mo, $1.25.
TWO MEN OF SANDY BAR. A Play. 18mo, $1.00.
THE STORY OF A MINE. 18mo, $1.00.
DRIFT FROM TWO SHORES. 18mo, $1.25.
THE TWINS OF TABLE MOUNTAIN, etc. 18mo, $1.25.
WORKS. New Edition. With Portrait. 5 vols. crown 8vo, each $2.00.
FLIP, AND FOUND AT BLAZING STAR. 18mo, $1.00.
IN THE CARQUINEZ WOODS. 18mo, $1.00.
ON THE FRONTIER. 18mo, $1.00.
BY SHORE AND SEDGE. 18mo, $1.00.
MARUJA. 18mo, $1.00.
SNOW-BOUND AT EAGLE'S. 18mo, $1.00.
A MILLIONAIRE OF ROUGH-AND-READY, AND DEVIL'S FORD. 18mo, $1.00.
THE LUCK OF ROARING CAMP, and other Stories. In Riverside Aldine Series. 16mo, $1.00.
THE QUEEN OF THE PIRATE ISLE. Illustrated by KATE GREENAWAY. 4to, $1.50.

HOUGHTON, MIFFLIN & CO., *Publishers,*
BOSTON AND NEW YORK.

A MILLIONAIRE OF ROUGH-AND-READY

AND DEVIL'S FORD

BY

BRET HARTE

BOSTON AND NEW YORK
HOUGHTON, MIFFLIN AND COMPANY
The Riverside Press, Cambridge
1887

Copyright, 1886 and 1887,
By BRET HARTE.

All rights reserved.

The Riverside Press, Cambridge:
Electrotyped and Printed by H. O. Houghton & Co.

CONTENTS.

———

	PAGE
A MILLIONAIRE OF ROUGH-AND-READY	5
DEVIL'S FORD	169

A MILLIONAIRE OF ROUGH-AND-READY.

PROLOGUE.

There was no mistake this time : he had struck gold at last!

It had lain there before him a moment ago — a misshapen piece of brown-stained quartz, interspersed with dull yellow metal; yielding enough to have allowed the points of his pick to penetrate its honeycombed recesses, .yet heavy enough to drop from the point of his pick as he endeavored to lift it from the red earth.

He was seeing all this plainly, although he found himself, he knew not why, at some distance from the scene of his discovery, his heart foolishly beating, his breath impotently hurried. Yet he was walking slowly and vaguely; conscious of stopping and staring at the landscape, which no longer looked familiar to him. He was hoping for some instinct or force of habit to recall him to himself; yet when he saw a neighbor at work in an adjacent claim, he hesitated, and then turned his back upon him. Yet only a moment before he had thought of running to him, saying, "By Jingo! I've struck it," or "D—n it, old man, I've got it;" but that moment had passed, and now it seemed to him that he could scarce raise his voice, or, if he did, the ejaculation would appear forced and artificial. Neither could he go over to him coolly and tell his good fortune; and, partly from this strange shyness, and partly with a hope that another survey of the treasure might restore him to natural expression, he walked back to his tunnel.

Yes; it was there! No mere "pocket" or "deposit," but a part of the actual vein he had been so long seeking. It was there, sure enough, lying beside the pick and the débris of the "face" of the vein that he had exposed sufficiently, after the first shock of discovery, to assure himself of the fact and the permanence of his fortune. It was there, and with it the refutation of his enemies' sneers, the corroboration of his friends' belief, the practical demonstration of his own theories, the reward of his patient labors. It was there, sure enough. But, somehow, he not only failed to recall the first joy of discovery, but was conscious of a vague sense of responsibility and unrest. It was, no doubt, an enormous fortune to a man in his circumstances : perhaps it meant a couple of hundred thousand dollars, or more, judging from the value of the old Martin lead, which was not as rich as this, but it required to be worked constantly and judiciously. It was with a decided sense of uneasiness that he again sought the open sunlight of the hillside. His neighbor was still visible on the adjacent claim; but he had apparently stopped working, and was contemplatively smoking a pipe under a large pine-tree. For an instant he envied him his apparent contentment. He had a sudden fierce and inexplicable desire to go over to him and exasperate his easy poverty by a revelation of his own new-found treasure. But even that sensation quickly passed, and left him staring blankly at the landscape again.

As soon as he had made his discovery known, and settled its value, he would send for his wife and her children in the States. He would build a fine house on the opposite hillside, if she would consent to it, unless she preferred, for the children's sake, to live in San Francisco. A sense of a loss of independence — of a change of circumstances that left him no longer his own master — began to perplex him, in the midst of his brightest projects. Certain other relations with other members of his family, which had lapsed by absence and his insignificance, must now be taken up anew. He must do something for his sister Jane, for his brother William, for his wife's poor connections. It would be unfair to him to say that he contemplated those things with any other instinct than that of generosity; yet he was conscious of being already perplexed and puzzled.

Meantime, however, the neighbor had apparently finished his pipe, and, knocking the ashes out of it, rose suddenly, and ended any further uncertainty of their meeting by walking over directly towards him. The treasure-finder advanced a few steps on his side, and then stopped irresolutely.

"Hollo, Slinn!" said the neighbor, confidently.

"Hollo, Masters," responded Slinn, faintly. From the sound of the two voices a stranger might have mistaken their relative condition. "What in thunder are you mooning about for? What's up?" Then, catching sight of Slinn's pale and anxious face, he added abruptly, "Are you sick?"

Slinn was on the point of telling him his good fortune, but stopped. The unlucky question confirmed his consciousness of his physical and mental disturbance, and he dreaded the ready ridicule of his companion. He would tell him later; Masters need not know *when* he had made the strike. Besides, in his present vagueness, he shrank from the brusque, practical questioning that would be sure to follow the revelation to a man of Masters' temperament.

"I'm a little giddy here," he answered, putting his hand to his head, "and I thought I'd knock off until I was better."

Masters examined him with two very critical gray eyes. "Tell ye what, old man!— if you don't quit this dog-goned foolin' of yours in that God-forsaken tunnel you'll get loony! Times you get so tangled up in follerin' that blind lead o' yours you ain't sensible!"

Here was the opportunity to tell him all, and vindicate the justice of his theories! But he shrank from it again; and now, adding to the confusion, was a singular sense of dread at the mental labor of explanation. He only smiled painfully, and began to move away. "Look you!" said Masters, peremptorily, " ye want about three fingers of straight whiskey to set you right, and you've got to take it with me. D—n it, man, it may be the last drink we take together! Don't look so skeered! I mean — I made up my mind about ten minutes ago to cut the whole d——d thing, and light out for fresh diggings. I'm sick of getting only grub wages out o' this hill. So that's what I mean by saying it's the last drink you and me 'll take together. You know my ways: sayin' and doin' with me 's the same thing."

It was true. Slinn had often envied Masters' promptness of decision and resolution. But he only looked at the grim face of his interlocutor with a feeble sense of relief. He was *going*. And he, Slinn, would not have to explain anything!

He murmured something about having to go over to the settlement on business. He dreaded lest Masters should insist upon going into the tunnel.

"I suppose you want to mail that letter," said Masters, drily. "The mail don't go till to-morrow, so you 've got time to finish it, and put it in an envelope."

Following the direction of Masters' eyes, Slinn looked down and saw, to his utter surprise, that he was holding an unfinished pencilled note in his hand. How it came there, when he had written it, he could not tell; he dimly remembered that one of his first impulses was to write to his wife, but that he had already done so he had forgotten. He hastily concealed the note in his breast-pocket, with a vacant smile. Masters eyed him half contemptuously, half compassionately.

"Don't forget yourself and drop it in some hollow tree for a letter-box," he said. "Well — so long! — since you won't drink. Take care of yourself," and, turning on his heel, Masters walked away.

Slinn watched him as he crossed over to his abandoned claim, saw him gather his few mining utensils, strap his blanket over his back, lift his hat on his long-handled shovel as a token of farewell, and then stride light-heartedly over the ridge.

He was alone now with his secret and his treasure. The only man in the world who knew of the exact position of his tunnel had gone away forever. It was not likely that this chance companion of a few weeks would ever remember him or the locality again; he would now leave his treasure alone — for even a day perhaps — until he had thought out some plan and sought out some friend in whom to confide. His secluded life, the singular habits of concentration which had at last proved so successful, had, at the same time, left him few acquaintances and no associates. And in all his well-laid plans and patiently-digested theories for finding the treasure, the means and methods of working it and disposing of it had never entered.

And now, at the hour when he most needed his faculties, what was the meaning of this strange benumbing of them!

Patience! He only wanted a little rest — a little time to recover himself. There was a large boulder under a tree in the highway to the settlement — a sheltered spot where he had often waited for the coming of the stage-coach. He would go there, and when he was sufficiently rested and composed he would go on.

Nevertheless, on his way he diverged and turned into the woods, for no other apparent purpose than to find a hollow tree. "A hollow tree." Yes! that was what Masters had said; he remembered it distinctly; and something was to be done there, but what it was, or why it should be done, he could not tell. However, it was done, and very luckily, for his limbs could scarcely support him further, and reaching that boulder he dropped upon it like another stone.

And now, strange to say, the uneasiness and perplexity which had possessed him ever since he had stood before his revealed wealth dropped from him like a burden laid upon the wayside. A measureless peace stole over him, in which visions of his new-found fortune, no longer a trouble and perplexity, but crowned with happiness and blessing to all around him, assumed proportions far beyond his own weak, selfish plans. In its even-handed benefaction, his wife and children, his friends and relations, even his late poor companion of the hillside, met and moved harmoniously together; in its far-reaching consequences there was only the influence of good. It was not strange that this poor finite mind should never have conceived the meaning of the wealth extended to him; or that conceiving it he should faint and falter under the revelation. Enough that for a few minutes he must have tasted a joy of perfect anticipation that years of actual possession might never bring.

The sun seemed to go down in a rosy dream of his own happiness, as he still sat there. Later, the shadows of the trees thickened and surrounded him, and still later fell the calm of a quiet evening sky with far-spaced passionless stars, that seemed as little troubled by what they looked upon as he was by the stealthy creeping life in the grasses and underbrush at his feet. The dull patter of soft little feet in the soft dust of the road, the gentle gleam of moist and wondering little eyes on the branches and in the mossy edges of the boulder, did not disturb him. He sat patiently through it all, as if he had not yet made up his mind.

But when the stage came with the flashing sun the next morning, and the irresistible clamor of life and action, the driver suddenly laid his four spirited horses on their haunches before the quiet spot. The express messenger clambered down from the box, and approached what seemed to be a heap of cast-off clothes upon the boulder.

"He don't seem to be drunk," he said, in reply to a querulous interrogation from the passengers. "I can't make him out. His eyes are open, but he cannot speak or move. Take a look at him, Doc."

A rough, unprofessional-looking man here descended from the inside of the coach, and, carelessly thrusting aside the other curious passengers, suddenly leant over the heap of clothes in a professional attitude.

"He is dead," said one of the passengers.

The rough man let the passive head sink softly down again. "No such luck for him," he said curtly, but not unkindly. "It's a stroke of paralysis — and about as big as they make 'em. It's a toss-up if he ever speaks or moves again as long as he lives."

CHAPTER I.

When Alvin Mulrady announced his intention of growing potatoes and garden "truck" on the green slopes of Los Gatos, the mining community of that region, and the adjacent hamlet of "Rough-and-Ready," regarded it with the contemptuous indifference usually shown by those adventurers towards all bucolic pursuits. There was certainly no active objection to the occupation of two hillsides, which gave so little promise to the prospector for gold that it was currently reported that a single prospector, called "Slinn," had once gone mad or imbecile through repeated failures. The only opposition came, incongruously enough, from the original pastoral owner of the soil, one Don Ramon Alvarado, whose claim for seven leagues of hill and valley, including the now prosperous towns of Rough-and-Ready and Red Dog, was met with simple derision from the squatters and miners. "Looks ez ef we woz goin' to travel three thousand miles to open up his d——d old wilderness, and then pay for the increased valoo we give it — don't it? Oh, yes, certainly!" was their ironical commentary. Mulrady might have been pardoned for adopting this popular opinion; but by an equally incongruous sentiment, peculiar, however, to the man, he called upon Don Ramon, and actually offered to purchase the land, or "go shares" with him in the agricultural profits. It was alleged that the Don was so struck with this concession that he not only granted the land, but struck up a quaint reserved friendship for the simple-minded agriculturist and his family. It is scarcely necessary to add that this intimacy was viewed by the miners with the contempt that it deserved. They would have been more contemptuous, however, had they known the opinion that Don Ramon entertained of their particular vocation, and which he early confided to Mulrady.

"They are savages, who expect to reap where they have not sown; to take out of the earth without returning anything to it but their precious carcasses; heathens, who worship the mere stones they dig up." "And was there no Spaniard who ever dug gold?" asked Mulrady, simply. "Ah, there are Spaniards and Moors," responded Don Ramon, sententiously. "Gold has been dug, and by caballeros; but no good ever came of it. There were Alvarados in Sonora, look you, who had mines of *silver*, and worked them with peons and mules, and lost their money — a gold mine to work a silver one — like gentlemen! But this grubbing in the dirt with one's fingers, that a little gold may stick to them, is not for caballeros. And then, one says nothing of the curse."

"The curse!" echoed Mary Mulrady, with youthful feminine superstition. "What is that?"

"You knew not, friend Mulrady, that when these lands were given to my ancestors by Charles V., the Bishop of Monterey laid a curse upon any who should desecrate them. Good! Let us see! Of the three Americanos who founded yonder town, one was shot, another died of a fever — poisoned, you understand, by the soil — and the last got himself crazy of aguardiente. Even the scientifico,[1] who came here years ago and spied into the trees and the herbs: he was afterwards punished for his profanation, and died of an accident in other lands. But," added Don Ramon, with grave courtesy, "this touches not yourself. Through me, *you* are of the soil."

Indeed, it would seem as if a secure if not a rapid prosperity was the result of Don Ramon's manorial patronage. The potato patch and market garden flourished exceedingly; the rich soil responded with magnificent vagaries of growth; the even sunshine set the seasons at defiance with extraordinary and premature crops. The salt pork and biscuit consuming settlers did not allow their contempt of Mulrady's occupation to prevent their profiting by this opportunity for chang-

---

[1] Don Ramon probably alluded to the eminent naturalist Douglas, who visited California before the gold excitement, and died of an accident in the Sandwich Islands.

ing their diet. The gold they had taken from the soil presently began to flow into his pockets in exchange for his more modest treasures. The little cabin, which barely sheltered his family — a wife, son, and daughter — was enlarged, extended, and refitted, but in turn abandoned for a more pretentious house on the opposite hill. A whitewashed fence replaced the rudely-split rails, which had kept out the wilderness. By degrees, the first evidences of cultivation — the gashes of red soil, the piles of brush and undergrowth, the bared boulders, and heaps of stone — melted away, and were lost under a carpet of lighter green, which made an oasis in the tawny desert of wild oats on the hillside. Water was the only free boon denied this Garden of Eden; what was necessary for irrigation had to be brought from a mining ditch at great expense, and was of insufficient quantity. In this emergency Mulrady thought of sinking an artesian well on the sunny slope beside his house; not, however, without serious consultation and much objection from his Spanish patron.

With great austerity Don Ramon pointed out that this trifling with the entrails of the earth was not only an indignity to Nature almost equal to shaft-sinking and tunnelling, but was a disturbance of vested interests. " I and my fathers, San Diego rest them!" said Don Ramon, crossing himself, " were content with wells and cisterns, filled by Heaven at its appointed seasons; the cattle, dumb brutes though they were, knew where to find water when they wanted it. But thou sayest truly," he added, with a sigh, " that was before streams and rain were choked with hellish engines, and poisoned with their spume. Go on, friend Mulrady, dig and bore if thou wilt, but in a seemly fashion, and not with impious earthquakes of devilish gunpowder."

With this concession Alvin Mulrady began to sink his first artesian shaft. Being debarred the auxiliaries of steam and gunpowder, the work went on slowly. The market garden did not suffer meantime, as Mulrady had employed two Chinamen to take charge of the ruder tillage, while he superintended the engineering work of the well. This trifling incident marked an epoch in the social condition of the family. Mrs. Mulrady at once assumed a conscious importance among her neighbors. She spoke of her husband's "men;" she alluded to the well as "the works;" she checked the easy frontier familiarity of her customers with pretty Mary Mulrady, her seventeen-year-old daughter. Simple Alvin Mulrady looked with astonishment at this sudden development of the germ planted in all feminine nature to expand in the slightest sunshine of prosperity. "Look yer, Malviny; ain't ye rather puttin' on airs with the boys that want to be civil to Mamie? Like as not one of 'em may be makin' up to her already." "You don't mean to say, Alvin Mulrady," responded Mrs. Mulrady, with sudden severity, "that you ever thought of givin' your daughter to a common miner, or that I'm goin' to allow her to marry out of our own set?" "Our own set!" echoed Mulrady feebly, blinking at her in astonishment, and then glancing hurriedly across at his freckle-faced son and the two Chinamen at work in the cabbages. "Oh, you know what I mean," said Mrs. Mulrady sharply; "the set that we move in. The Alvarados and their friends! Doesn't the old Don come here every day, and ain't his son the right age for Mamie? And ain't they the real first families here — all the same as if they were noblemen? No, leave Mamie to me, and keep to your shaft; there never was a man yet had the least *sabe* about these things, or knew what was due to his family." Like most of his larger minded, but feebler equipped sex, Mulrady was too glad to accept the truth of the latter proposition, which left the meannesses of life to feminine manipulation, and went off to his shaft on the hillside. But during that afternoon he was perplexed and troubled. He was too loyal a husband not to be pleased with this proof of an unexpected and superior foresight in his wife, although he was, like all husbands, a little startled by it. He tried to dismiss it from his mind. But looking down from the hillside upon his little venture, where gradual increase and prosperity had not been beyond his faculties to control and understand, he found himself haunted by the more ambitious projects of his helpmate. From his own knowledge of men, he doubted if Don Ramon, any more than himself, had ever thought of the possibility of a matrimonial connection between the families. He doubted if he would consent to it. And unfortunately it was this very doubt that, touching his own pride as a self-made man, made him first seriously consider his wife's proposition. He was as good as Don Ramon, any day! With this subtle feminine poison instilled in his veins, carried completely away by the logic of his wife's illogical premises, he almost hated his old benefactor. He looked down upon the little Garden of Eden, where his Eve had just tempted him with the fatal fruit, and felt a curious consciousness that he was losing its simple and innocent enjoyment forever.

Happily, about this time Don Ramon died. It is not probable that he ever knew the amiable intentions of Mrs. Mulrady in regard to his son, who now succeeded to the paternal estate, sadly partitioned by relatives and lawsuits. The feminine Mulradys attended the funeral, in expensive mourning from Sacramento; even the gentle Alvin was forced into ready-made broadcloth, which accented his good-natured but unmistakably common presence. Mrs. Mulrady spoke openly of her "loss;" declared that the old families were dying out; and impressed the wives of a few new arrivals at Red Dog with the belief that her own family was contemporary with the Alvarados, and that her husband's health was far from perfect. She extended a motherly sympathy to the orphaned Don Cæsar. Reserved, like his father, in natural disposition, he was still more gravely ceremonious from his loss; and, perhaps from the shyness of an evident partiality for Mamie Mulrady, he rarely availed himself of her mother's sympathizing hospitality. But he carried out the intentions of his father by consenting to sell to Mulrady, for a small sum, the property he had leased. The idea of purchasing had originated with Mrs. Mulrady.

"It'll be all in the family," had observed that astute lady, "and it's better for the looks of the things that we should n't be his tenants."

It was only a few weeks later that she was startled by hearing her husband's voice calling her from the hillside as he rapidly approached the house. Mamie was in her room putting on a new pink cotton gown, in honor of an expected visit from young Don Cæsar, and Mrs. Mulrady was tidying the house in view of the same event. Something in the tone of her good man's voice, and the unusual circumstance of his return to the house before work was done, caused her, however, to drop her dusting cloth, and run to the kitchen door to meet him. She saw him running through the rows of cabbages, his face shining with perspiration and excitement, a light in his eyes which she had not seen for years. She recalled, without sentiment, that he looked like that when she had called him — a poor farm hand of her father's — out of the brush heap at the back of their former home, in Illinois, to learn the consent of her parents. The recollection was the more embarrassing as he threw his arms around her, and pressed a resounding kiss upon her sallow cheek.

"Sakes alive! Mulrady!" she said, exorcising the ghost of a blush that had also been recalled from the past with her housewife's apron, "what are you doin', and company expected every minit?"

"Malviny, I've struck it; and struck it rich!"

She disengaged herself from his arms, without excitement, and looked at him with bright but shrewdly observant eyes.

"I've struck it in the well — the regular vein that the boys have been looking fer. There's a fortin' fer you and Mamie: thousands and tens of thousands!"

"Wait a minit."

She left him quickly, and went to the foot of the stairs. He could hear her wonderingly and distinctly. "Ye can take off that new frock, Mamie," she called out.

There was a sound of undisguised expostulation from Mamie.

"I'm speaking," said Mrs. Mulrady, emphatically.

The murmuring ceased. Mrs. Mulrady returned to her husband. The interruption seemed to have taken off the keen edge of his enjoyment. He at once abdicated his momentary elevation as a discoverer, and waited for her to speak.

"Ye haven't told any one yet?" she asked.

"No. I was alone, down in the shaft. Ye see, Malviny, I wasn't expectin' of anything." He began, with an attempt at fresh enjoyment, "I was just clearin' out, and hadn't reckoned on anythin'."

"You see, I was right when I advised your taking the land," she said, without heeding him.

Mulrady's face fell. "I hope Don Cæsar won't think" — he began, hesitatingly. "I reckon, perhaps, I oughter make some sorter compensation — you know."

"Stuff!" said Mrs. Mulrady, decidedly. "Don't be a fool. Any gold discovery, anyhow, would have been yours — that's the law. And you bought the land without any restrictions. Besides, you never had any idea of this!" — she stopped, and looked him suddenly in the face — "had you?"

Mulrady opened his honest, pale-gray eyes widely.

"Why, Malviny! You know I had n't. I could swear!"

"Don't swear, and don't let on to anybody but what you *did* know it was there. Now, Alvin Mulrady, listen to me." Her voice here took the strident form of action. "Knock off work at the shaft, and send your man away at once. Put on your things, catch the next stage to Sacramento at four o'clock, and take Mamie with you."

"Mamie!" echoed Mulrady, feebly.

"You want to see Lawyer Cole and my brother Jim at once," she went on, without heeding him, "and Mamie wants a change and some proper clothes. Leave the rest to me and Abner. I 'll break it to Mamie, and get her ready."

Mulrady passed his hands through his tangled hair, wet with perspiration. He was proud of his wife's energy and action; he did not dream of opposing her, but somehow he was disappointed. The charming glamour and joy of his discovery had vanished before he could fairly dazzle her with it; or, rather, she was not dazzled with it at all. It had become like business, and the expression "breaking it" to Mamie jarred upon him. He would have preferred to tell her himself; to watch the color come into her delicate oval face, to have seen her soft eyes light with an innocent joy he had not seen in his wife's; and he felt a sinking conviction that his wife was the last one to awaken it.

"You ain't got any time to lose," she said, impatiently, as he hesitated.

Perhaps it was her impatience that struck harshly upon him; perhaps, if she had not accepted her good fortune so confidently, he would not have spoken what was in his mind at the time; but he said, gravely, "Wait a minit, Malviny; I've suthin' to tell you 'bout this find of mine that's sing'lar."

"Go on," she said, quickly.

"Lyin' among the rotten quartz of the vein was a pick," he said, constrainedly; "and the face of the vein sorter looked ez if it had been worked at. Follering the line outside to the base of the hill there was signs of there having been an old tunnel; but it had fallen in, and was blocked up."

"Well?" said Mrs. Mulrady, contemptuously.

"Well," returned her husband, somewhat disconnectedly, "it kinder looked as if some feller might have discovered it before."

"And went away, and left it for others! That's likely — ain't it?" interrupted his wife, with ill-disguised intolerance. "Everybody knows the hill was n't worth that for prospectin'; and it was abandoned when we came here. It's your property and you've paid for it. Are you goin' to wait to advertise for the owner, Alvin Mulrady, or are you going to Sacramento at four o'clock today?"

Mulrady started. He had never seriously believed in the possibility of a previous discovery; but his conscientious nature had prompted him to give it a fair consideration. She was probably right. What he might have thought had she treated it with equal conscientiousness he did not consider. "All right," he said simply. "I reckon we'll go at once."

"And when you talk to Lawyer Cole and Jim, keep that silly stuff about the pick to yourself. There's no use of putting queer ideas into other people's heads because you happen to have 'em yourself."

When the hurried arrangements were at last completed, and Mr. Mulrady and Mamie, accompanied by a taciturn and discreet Chinaman, carrying their scant luggage, were on their way to the high road to meet the up stage, the father gazed somewhat anxiously and wistfully into his daughter's face. He had looked forward to those few moments to enjoy the freshness and *naïveté* of Mamie's youthful delight and enthusiasm as a relief to his wife's practical, far-sighted realism. There was a pretty pink suffusion in her delicate cheek, the breathless happiness of a child in her half-opened little mouth, and a beautiful absorption in her large gray eyes that augured well for him.

"Well, Mamie, how do we like bein' an heiress? How do we like layin' over all the gals between this and 'Frisco?"

"Eh?"

She had not heard him. The tender beautiful eyes were engaged in an anticipatory examination of the remembered shelves in the "Fancy Emporium" at Sacramento; in reading the admiration of the clerks; in glancing down a little criticisingly at the broad cowhide brogues that strode at her side; in looking up the road for the stage-coach; in regarding the fit of her new gloves — everywhere but in the loving eyes of the man beside her.

He, however, repeated the question, touched with her charming preoccupation, and passing his arm around her little waist.

"I like it well enough, pa, you know!" she said, slightly disengaging his arm, but adding a perfunctory little squeeze to his elbow to soften the separation. "I always had an idea *something* would happen. I suppose I'm looking like a fright," she added; "but ma made me hurry to get away before Don Cæsar came."

"And you did n't want to go without seeing him?" he added, archly.

"I did n't want him to see me in this frock," said Mamie, simply. "I reckon that's why ma made me change," she added, with a slight laugh.

"Well, I reckon you're allus good enough for him in any dress," said Mulrady, watching her attentively; "and more than a match for him *now*," he added, triumphantly.

"I don't know about that," said Mamie. "He's been rich all the time, and his father and grandfather before him; while we've been poor and his tenants."

His face changed; the look of bewilderment, with which he had followed her words, gave way to one of pain, and then of anger. "Did he get off such stuff as that?" he asked, quickly.

"No. I'd like to catch him at it," responded Mamie, promptly. "There's better nor him to be had for the asking now."

They had walked on a few moments in aggrieved silence, and the Chinaman might have imagined some misfortune had just befallen them. But Mamie's teeth shone again between her parted lips. "La, pa! it ain't that! He cares everything for me, and I do for him; and if ma had n't got new ideas"— She stopped suddenly.

"What new ideas?" queried her father, anxiously.

"Oh, nothing! I wish, pa, you'd put on your other boots! Everybody can see these are made for the farrows. And you ain't a market gardener any more."

"What am I, then?" asked Mulrady, with a half-pleased, half-uneasy laugh.

"You're a capitalist, *I* say; but ma says a landed proprietor." Nevertheless, the landed proprietor, when he reached the boulder on the Red Dog highway, sat down in somewhat moody contemplation, with his head bowed over the broad cowhide brogues, that seemed to have already gathered enough of the soil to indicate his right to that title. Mamie, who had recovered her spirits, but had not lost her preoccupation, wandered off by herself in the meadow, or ascended the hillside, as her occasional impatience at the delay of the coach, or the following of some ambitious fancy, alternately prompted her. She was so far away at one time that the stage-coach, which finally drew up before Mulrady, was obliged to wait for her.

When she was deposited safely inside, and Mulrady had climbed to the box beside the driver, the latter remarked, curtly, —

"Ye gave me a right smart skeer, a minit ago, stranger."

"Ez how?"

"Well, about three years ago, I was comin' down this yer grade, at just this time, and sittin' right on that stone, in just your attitude, was a man about your build and years. I pulled up to let him in, when, darn my skin! if he ever moved, but sorter looked at me without speakin'. I called to him, and he never answered, 'cept with that idiotic stare. I then let him have my opinion of him, in mighty strong English, and drove off, leavin' him there. The next morning, when I came by on the up-trip, darn my skin! if he wasn't thar, but lyin' all of a heap on the boulder. Jim drops down and picks him up. Doctor Duchesne, ez was along, allowst it was a played-out prospector, with a big case of paralysis, and we expressed him through to the County Hospital, like so much dead freight. I've allus been kinder superstitious about passin' that rock, and when I saw you jist now, sittin' thar, dazed like, with your head down like the other chap, it rather threw me off my centre."

In the inexplicable and half-superstitious uneasiness that this coincidence awakened in Mulrady's unimaginative mind, he was almost on the point of disclosing his good fortune to the driver, in order to prove how preposterous was the parallel, but checked himself in time.

"Did you find out who he was?" broke in a rash passenger. "Did you ever get over it?" added another unfortunate.

With a pause of insulting scorn at the interruption, the driver resumed, pointedly, to

Mulrady: " The pint of the whole thing was my cussin' a helpless man, ez could neither cuss back nor shoot; and then afterwards takin' you for his ghost layin' for me to get even." He paused again, and then added, carelessly, " They say he never kem to enuff to let on who he was or whar he kem from ; and he was eventooally taken to a 'Sylum for Doddering Idjits and Gin'ral and Permiskus Imbeciles at Sacramento. I 've heerd it 's considered a first-class institooshun, not only for them ez is paralyzed and can't talk, as for them ez is the reverse and is too chipper. Now," he added, languidly turning for the first time to his miserable questioners, " how did *you* find it ? "

CHAPTER II.

When the news of the discovery of gold in Mulrady shaft was finally made public, it created an excitement hitherto unknown in the history of the country. Half of Red Dog and all Rough-and-Ready were emptied upon the yellow hills surrounding Mulrady's, until their circling camp fires looked like a besieging army that had invested his peaceful pastoral home, preparatory to carrying it by assault. Unfortunately for them, they found the various points of vantage already garrisoned with notices of "preëmption" for mining purposes in the name of the various members of the Alvarado family. This stroke of business was due to Mrs. Mulrady, as a means of mollifying the conscientious scruples of her husband and of placating the Alvarados, in view of some remote contingency. It is but fair to say that this degradation of his father's Castilian principles was opposed by Don Cæsar. "You need n't work them yourself, but sell out to them that will; it's the only way to keep the prospectors from taking it without paying for it at all," argued Mrs. Mulrady. Don Cæsar finally assented; perhaps less to the business arguments of Mulrady's wife than to the simple suggestion of Mamie's mother. Enough that he realized a sum in money for a few acres that exceeded the last ten years' income of Don Ramon's seven leagues.

Equally unprecedented and extravagant was the realization of the discovery in Mulrady's shaft. It was alleged that a company, hastily formed in Sacramento, paid him a million of dollars down, leaving him still a controlling two thirds interest in the mine. With an obstinacy, however, that amounted almost to a moral conviction, he refused to include the house and potato-patch in the property. When the company had yielded the point, he declined, with equal tenacity, to part with it to outside speculators on even the most extravagant offers. In vain Mrs. Mulrady protested; in vain she pointed out to him that the retention of the evidence of his former humble occupation was a green blot upon their social escutcheon.

"If you will keep the land, build on it, and root up the garden." But Mulrady was adamant.

"It's the only thing I ever made myself, and got out of the soil with my own hands; it's the beginning of my fortune, and it may be the end of it. Mebbee I'll be glad enough to have it to come back to some day, and be thankful for the square meal I can dig out of it."

By repeated pressure, however, Mulrady yielded the compromise that a portion of it should be made into a vineyard and flower-garden, and by a suitable coloring of ornament and luxury obliterate its vulgar part. Less successful, however, was that energetic woman in another effort to mitigate the austerities of their earlier state. It occurred to her to utilize the softer accents of Don Cæsar in the pronunciation of their family name, and privately had "Mulrade" take the place of Mulrady on her visiting card.

"It might be Spanish," she argued with her husband. " Lawyer Cole says most American names are corrupted, and how do you know that yours ain't?" Mulrady, who would not swear that his ancestors came from Ireland to the Carolinas in '98, was helpless to refute the assertion. But the terrible Nemesis of an un-Spanish, American provincial speech avenged the orthographical outrage at once. When Mrs. Mulrady began to be addressed orally, as well as by letter, as " Mrs. Mulraid," and when simple amatory effusions to her daughter rhymed with "lovely maid," she promptly restored the original vowel. But she fondly clung to the Spanish courtesy which transformed her husband's baptismal name, and usually spoke of him — in his absence — as " Don Alvino." But in the presence of his short, square figure, his orange tawny hair, his twinkling gray eyes, and *retroussé* nose, even that dominant woman withheld his title. It was currently reported at Red Dog that a distinguished foreigner had one day approached Mulrady with the formula, " I believe I have the honor of addressing Don Alvino Mulrady?" "You kin bet your boots, stranger, that's me," had returned that simple hidalgo.

Although Mrs. Mulrady would have preferred that Mamie should remain at Sacramento until she could join her, preparatory to a trip to "the States" and Europe, she yielded to her daughter's desire to astonish Rough-and-Ready, before she left, with her new wardrobe, and unfold in the parent nest the delicate and painted wings with which she was to fly from them forever. "I don't want them to remember me afterwards in those spotted prints, ma, and like as not say I never had a decent frock until I went away." There was something so like the daughter of her mother in this delicate foresight that the touched and gratified parent kissed her, and assented. The result was gratifying beyond her expectation. In that few weeks' sojourn at Sacramento, the young girl seemed to have adapted and assimilated herself to the latest modes of fashion with even more than the usual American girl's pliancy and taste. Equal to all emergencies of style and material, she seemed to supply, from some hitherto unknown quality she possessed, the grace and manner peculiar to each. Untrammeled by tradition, education, or precedent, she had the Western girl's confidence in all things being possible, which made them so often probable. Mr. Mulrady looked at his daughter with mingled sentiments of pride and awe. Was it possible that this delicate creature, so superior to him that he seemed like a degenerate scion of her remoter race, was his own flesh and blood? Was she the daughter of her mother, who even in her remembered youth was never equipped like this? If the thought brought no pleasure to his simple, loving nature, it at least spared him the pain of what might have seemed ingratitude in one more akin to himself. "The fact is, we ain't quite up to her style," was his explanation and apology. A vague belief that in another and a better world than this he might approximate and understand this perfection somewhat soothed and sustained him.

It was quite consistent, therefore, that the embroidered cambric dress which Mamie Mulrady wore one summer afternoon on the hillside at Los Gatos, while to the critical feminine eye at once artistic and expensive, should not seem incongruous to her surroundings or to herself in the eyes of a general audience. It certainly did not seem so to one pair of frank, humorous ones that glanced at her from time to time, as their owner, a young fellow of five-and-twenty, walked at her side. He was the new editor of the "Rough-and-Ready Record," and, having been her fellow-passenger from Sacramento, had already once or twice availed himself of her father's invitation to call upon them. Mrs. Mulrady had not discouraged this mild flirtation. Whether she wished to disconcert Don Cæsar for some occult purpose, or whether, like the rest of her sex, she had an overweening confidence in the unheroic, unseductive, and purely platonic character of masculine humor, did not appear.

"When I say I'm sorry you are going to

leave us, Miss Mulrady," said the young fellow, lightly, "you will comprehend my unselfishness, since I frankly admit your departure would be a positive relief to me as an editor and a man. The pressure in the Poet's Corner of the 'Record' since it was mistakingly discovered that a person of your name might be induced to seek the 'glade' and 'shade' without being 'afraid,' 'dismayed,' or 'betrayed,' has been something enormous, and, unfortunately, I am debarred from rejecting anything, on the just ground that I am myself an interested admirer."

"It is dreadful to be placarded around the country by one's own full name, is n't it?" said Mamie, without, however, expressing much horror in her face.

"They think it much more respectful than to call you 'Mamie,'" he responded, lightly; "and many of your admirers are middle-aged men, with a mediæval style of compliment. I've discovered that amatory versifying was n't entirely a youthful passion. Colonel Cash is about as fatal with a couplet as with a double-barreled gun, and scatters as terribly. Judge Butts and Dr. Wilson have both discerned the resemblance of your gifts to those of Venus, and their own to Apollo. But don't undervalue those tributes, Miss Mulrady," he added, more seriously. "You'll have thousands of admirers where you are going; but you'll be willing to admit in the end, I think, that none were more honest and respectful than your subjects at Rough-and-Ready and Red Dog." He stopped, and added in a graver tone, "Does Don Cæsar write poetry?"

"He has something better to do," said the young lady, pertly.

"I can easily imagine that," he returned, mischievously; "it must be a pallid substitute for other opportunities."

"What did you come here for?" she asked, suddenly.

"To see you."

"Nonsense! You know what I mean. Why did you ever leave Sacramento to come here? I should think it would suit you so much better than this place."

"I suppose I was fired by your father's example, and wished to find a gold mine."

"Men like you never do," she said, simply.

"Is that a compliment, Miss Mulrady?"

"I don't know. But I think that you think that it is."

He gave her the pleased look of one who had unexpectedly found a sympathetic intelligence. "Do I? This is interesting. Let's sit down." In their desultory rambling they had reached, quite unconsciously, the large boulder at the roadside. Mamie hesitated a moment, looked up and down the road, and then, with an already opulent indifference to the damaging of her spotless skirt, sat herself upon it, with her furled parasol held by her two little hands thrown over her half-drawn-up knee. The young editor, half sitting, half leaning, against the stone, began to draw figures in the sand with his cane.

"On the contrary, Miss Mulrady, I hope to make some money here. You are leaving Rough-and-Ready because you are rich. We are coming to it because we are poor."

"We?" echoed Mamie, lazily, looking up the road.

"Yes. My father and two sisters."

"I am sorry. I might have known them if I hadn't been going away." At the same moment, it flashed across her mind that, if they were like the man before her, they might prove disagreeably independent and critical. "Is your father in business?" she asked.

He shook his head. After a pause, he said, punctuating his sentences with the point of his stick in the soft dust, "He is paralysed, and out of his mind, Miss Mulrady. I came to California to seek him, as all news of him ceased three years since; and I found him only two weeks ago, alone, friendless — an unrecognized pauper in the county hospital."

"Two weeks ago? That was when I went to Sacramento."

"Very probably."

"It must have been very shocking to you?"

"It was."

"I should think you'd feel real bad?"

"I do, at times." He smiled, and laid his stick on the stone. "You now see, Miss Mulrady, how necessary to me is this good fortune that you don't think me worthy of. Meantime I must try to make a home for them at Rough-and-Ready."

Miss Mulrady put down her knee and her parasol. " We must n't stay here much longer, you know."

" Why ? "

" Why, the stage-coach comes by at about this time."

" And you think the passengers will observe us sitting here ? "

" Of course they will."

" Miss Mulrady, I implore you to stay."

He was leaning over her with such apparent earnestness of voice and gesture that the color came into her cheek. For a moment she scarcely dared to lift her conscious eyes to his. When she did so, she suddenly glanced her own aside with a flash of anger. He was laughing.

" If you have any pity for me, do not leave me now," he repeated. " Stay a moment longer, and my fortune is made. The passengers will report us all over Red Dog as engaged. I shall be supposed to be in your father's secrets, and shall be sought after as a director of all the new companies. The 'Record' will double its circulation; poetry will drop out of its columns, advertising rush to fill its place, and I shall receive five dollars a week more salary, if not seven and a half. Never mind the consequences to yourself at such a moment. I assure you there will be none. You can deny it the next day — *I* will deny it — nay, more, the 'Record' itself will deny it in an extra edition of one thousand copies, at ten cents each. Linger a moment longer, Miss Mulrady. Fly, oh fly not yet. They're coming — hark! ho! By Jove, it's only Don Cæsar!"

It was, indeed, only the young scion of the house of Alvarado, blue-eyed, sallow-skinned, and high-shouldered, coming towards them on a fiery, half-broken mustang, whose very spontaneous lawlessness seemed to accentuate and bring out the grave and decorous ease of his rider. Even in his burlesque preoccupation the editor of the "Record" did not withhold his admiration of this perfect horsemanship. Mamie, who, in her wounded *amour propre*, would like to have made much of it to annoy her companion, was thus estopped any ostentatious compliment.

Don Cæsar lifted his hat with sweet seriousness to the lady, with grave courtesy to the gentleman. While the lower half of this Centaur was apparently quivering with fury, and stamping the ground in his evident desire to charge upon the pair, the upper half, with natural dignity, looked from the one to the other, as if to leave the privilege of an explanation with them. But Mamie was too wise, and her companion too indifferent, to offer one. A slight shade passed over Don Cæsar's face. To complicate the situation at that moment, the expected stage-coach came rattling by. With quick feminine intuition, Mamie caught in the faces of the driver and the expressman, and reflected in the mischievous eyes of her companion, a peculiar interpretation of their meeting, that was not removed by the whispered assurance of the editor that the passengers were anxiously looking back " to see the shooting."

The young Spaniard, equally oblivious of humor or curiosity, remained impassive.

"You know Mr. Slinn, of the 'Record,'" said Mamie, "don't you?"

Don Cæsar had never before met the Señor Esslinn. He was under the impression that it was a Señor Robinson that was of the "Record."

"Oh! *he* was shot," said Slinn. "I'm taking his place."

"Bueno! To be shot too? I trust not."

Slinn looked quickly and sharply into Don Cæsar's grave face. He seemed to be incapable of any double meaning. However, as he had no serious reason for awakening Don Cæsar's jealousy, and very little desire to become an embarrassing third in this conversation, and possibly a burden to the young lady, he proceeded to take his leave of her. From a sudden feminine revulsion of sympathy, or from some unintelligible instinct of diplomacy, Mamie said, as she extended her hand, "I hope you'll find a home for your family near here. Mamma wants pa to let our old house. Perhaps it might suit you, if not too far from your work. You might speak to ma about it."

"Thank you; I will," responded the young man, pressing her hand with unaffected cordiality.

Don Cæsar watched him until he had disappeared behind the wayside buckeyes.

"He is a man of family — this one — your countryman?"

It seemed strange to her to have a mere acquaintance spoken of as "her countryman" — not the first time nor the last time in her career. As there appeared no trace or sign of jealousy in her questioner's manner, she answered briefly but vaguely.

"Yes; it's a shocking story. His father disappeared some years ago, and he has just found him — a helpless paralytic — in the Sacramento Hospital. He'll have to support him — and they're very poor."

"So, then, they are not independent of each other always — these fathers and children of Americans!"

"No," said Mamie, shortly. Without knowing why, she felt inclined to resent Don

Cæsar's manner. His serious gravity — gentle and high-bred as it was, undoubtedly — was somewhat trying to her at times, and seemed even more so after Slinn's irreverent humor. She picked up her parasol, a little impatiently, as if to go.

But Don Cæsar had already dismounted, and tied his horse to a tree with a strong lariat that hung at his saddle-bow.

"Let us walk through the woods towards your home. I can return alone for the horse when you shall dismiss me."

They turned in among the pines that, overcrowding the hollow, crept partly up the side of the hill of Mulrady's shaft. A disused trail, almost hidden by the waxen-hued yerba buena, led from the highway, and finally lost itself in the undergrowth. It was a lovers' walk; they were lovers, evidently, and yet the man was too self-poised in his gravity, the young woman too conscious and critical, to suggest an absorbing or oblivious passion.

"I should not have made myself so obtrusive to-day before your friend," said Don

Cæsar, with proud humility, "but I could not understand from your mother whether you were alone or whether my company was desirable. It is of this I have now to speak, Mamie. Lately your mother has seemed strange to me; avoiding any reference to our affection; treating it lightly, and even as to-day, I fancy, putting obstacles in the way of our meeting alone. She was disappointed at your return from Sacramento, where, I have been told, she intended you to remain until you left the country; and since your return I have seen you but twice. I may be wrong. Perhaps I do not comprehend the American mother; I have — who knows? — perhaps offended in some point of etiquette, omitted some ceremony that was her due. But when you told me, Mamie, that it was not necessary to speak to *her* first, that it was not the American fashion" —

Mamie started, and blushed slightly.

"Yes," she said hurriedly, "certainly; but ma has been quite queer of late, and she may think — you know — that since —

since there has been so much property to dispose of, she ought to have been consulted."

"Then let us consult her at once, dear child! And as to the property, in Heaven's name, let her dispose of it as she will. Saints forbid that an Alvarado should ever interfere. And what is it to us, my little one? Enough that Doña Mameta Alvarado will never have less state than the richest bride that ever came to Los Gatos."

Mamie had not forgotten that, scarcely a month ago, even had she loved the man before her no more than she did at present, she would still have been thrilled with delight at these words! Even now she was moved — conscious as she had become that the "state" of a bride of the Alvarados was not all she had imagined, and that the bare adobe court of Los Gatos was open to the sky and the free criticism of Sacramento capitalists!

"Yes, dear," she murmured, with a half childlike pleasure, that lit up her face and eyes so innocently that it stopped any minute investigation into its origin and real meaning. "Yes, dear; but we need not have a fuss made about it at present, and perhaps put ma against us. She would n't hear of our marrying now; and she might forbid our engagement."

"But you are going away."

"I should have to go to New York or Europe *first*, you know," she answered, naively, "even if it were all settled. I should have to get things! One could n't be decent here."

With the recollection of the pink cotton gown, in which she had first pledged her troth to him, before his eyes, he said, "But you are charming now. You cannot be more so to me. If I am satisfied, little one, with you as you are, let us go together, and then you can get dresses to please others."

She had not expected this importunity. Really, if it came to this, she might have engaged herself to some one like Slinn; he at least would have understood her. He was much cleverer, and certainly more of a man of the world. When Slinn had treated her like a child, it was with the humorous tolerance of an admiring superior, and not the didactic impulse of a guardian. She did not say this, nor did her pretty eyes indicate it, as in the instance of her brief anger with Slinn. She only said gently, —

"I should have thought you, of all men, would have been particular about your wife doing the proper thing. But never mind! Don't let us talk any more about it. Perhaps, as it seems such a great thing to you, and so much trouble, there may be no necessity for it at all."

I do not think that the young lady deliberately planned this charmingly illogical deduction from Don Cæsar's speech, or that she calculated its effect upon him; but it was part of her nature to say it, and profit by it. Under the unjust lash of it, his pride gave way.

"Ah, do you not see why I wish to go with you?" he said, with sudden and unexpected passion. "You are beautiful; you are good; it has pleased Heaven to make you rich also; but you are a child in experience, and know not your own heart. With your beauty, your goodness, and your wealth, you will attract all to you — as you do here — because you cannot help it. But you will be equally helpless, little one, if *they* should attract *you*, and you had no tie to fall back upon."

It was an unfortunate speech. The words were Don Cæsar's; but the thought she had heard before from her mother, although the deduction had been of a very different kind. Mamie followed the speaker with bright but visionary eyes. There must be some truth in all this. Her mother had said it; Mr. Slinn had laughingly admitted it. She *had* a brilliant future before her! Was she right in making it impossible by a rash and foolish tie? He himself had said she was inexperienced. She knew it; and yet, what was he doing now but taking advantage of that inexperience? If he really loved her, he would be willing to submit to the test. She did not ask a similar one from him; and was willing, if she came out of it free, to marry him just' the same. There was something so noble in this thought that she felt for a moment carried away by an impulse of compassionate unselfishness, and smiled tenderly as she looked up in his face.

"Then you consent, Mamie?" he said, eagerly, passing his arm around her waist.

"Not now, Cæsar," she said, gently disengaging herself. "I must think it over; we are both too young to act upon it rashly; it would be unfair to you, who are so quiet and have seen so few girls — I mean Americans — to tie yourself to the first one you have known. When I am gone you will go more into the world. There are Mr. Slinn's two sisters coming here — I should n't wonder if they were far cleverer and talked far better than I do — and think how I should feel if I knew that only a wretched pledge to me kept you from loving them!" She stopped, and cast down her eyes.

It was her first attempt at coquetry, for, in her usual charming selfishness, she was perfectly frank and open; and it might not have been her last, but she had gone too far at first, and was not prepared for a recoil of her own argument.

"If you admit that it is possible — that it is possible to you!" he said, quickly.

She saw her mistake. "We may not have many opportunities to meet alone," she answered, quietly; "and I am sure we would be happier when we meet not to accuse each other of impossibilities. Let us rather see how we can communicate together, if anything should prevent our meeting. Remember, it was only by chance that you were able to see me now. If ma has believed that she ought to have been consulted, our meeting together in this secret way will only make matters worse. She is even now wondering where I am, and may be suspicious. I must go back at once. At any moment some one may come here looking for me."

"But I have so much to say," he pleaded. "Our time has been so short."

"You can write."

"But what will your mother think of that?" he said, in grave astonishment.

She colored again as she returned, quickly, "Of course, you must not write to the house. You can leave a letter somewhere for me —

say, somewhere about here. Stop!" she added, with a sudden girlish gayety, " see, here's the very place. Look there!"

She pointed to the decayed trunk of a blasted sycamore, a few feet from the trail. A cavity, breast high, half filled with skeleton leaves and pine-nuts, showed that it had formerly been a squirrel's hoard, but for some reason had been deserted.

"Look! it's a regular letter-box," she continued, gayly, rising on tip-toe to peep into its recesses. Don Cæsar looked at her admiringly; it seemed like a return to their first idyllic love-making in the old days, when she used to steal out of the cabbage rows in her brown linen apron and sun-bonnet to walk with him in the woods. He recalled the fact to her with the fatality of a lover already seeking to restore in past recollections something that was wanting in the present. She received it with the impatience of youth, to whom the present is all sufficient.

"I wonder how you could ever have cared for me in that holland apron," she said, looking down upon her new dress.

"Shall I tell you why?" he said, fondly, passing his arm around her waist, and drawing her pretty head nearer his shoulder.

"No — not now!" she said, laughingly, but struggling to free herself. "There's not time. Write it, and put it in the box. There," she added, hastily, "listen! — what's that?"

"It's only a squirrel," he whispered reassuringly in her ear.

"No; it's somebody coming! I must go! Please! Cæsar, dear! There, then" —

She met his kiss half-way, released herself with a lithe movement of her wrist and shoulder, and the next moment seemed to slip into the woods, and was gone.

Don Cæsar listened with a sigh as the last rustling ceased, cast a look at the decayed tree as if to fix it in his memory, and then slowly retraced his steps towards his tethered mustang.

He was right, however, in his surmise of the cause of that interruption. A pair of bright eyes had been watching them from the bough of an adjacent tree. It was a squirrel, who, having had serious and prior intentions of making use of the cavity they had discovered, had only withheld examination by an apparent courteous discretion towards the intruding pair. Now that they were gone he slipped down the tree and ran towards the decayed stump.

CHAPTER III.

APPARENTLY dissatisfied with the result of an investigation, which proved that the cavity was unfit as a treasure hoard for a discreet squirrel, whatever its value as a receptacle for the love-tokens of incautious humanity, the little animal at once set about to put things in order. He began by whisking out an immense quantity of dead leaves, disturbed a family of tree-spiders, dissipated a drove of patient aphides browsing in the bark, as well as their attendant dairymen, the ants, and otherwise ruled it with the high hand of dispossession and a contemptuous opinion of the previous incumbents. It must not be supposed, however, that his proceedings were altogether free from contemporaneous criticism; a venerable crow sitting on a branch above him displayed great interest in his occupation, and, hopping down a few moments afterwards, disposed of some worm-eaten nuts, a few larvæ, and an insect or two, with languid dignity and without prejudice. Certain incumbrances, however, still resisted the squirrel's general eviction; among them a folded square of paper with sharply defined edges, that declined investigation, and, owing to a nauseous smell of tobacco, escaped nibbling as it had apparently escaped insect ravages. This, owing to its sharp angles, which persisted in catching in the soft decaying wood in his whirlwind of house-cleaning, he allowed to remain. Having thus, in a general way, prepared for the coming winter, the self-satisfied little rodent dismissed the subject from his active mind.

His rage and indignation a few days later may be readily conceived, when he found, on returning to his new-made home, another square of paper, folded like the first, but much fresher and whiter, lying within the cavity, on top of some moss which had evidently been placed there for the purpose. This he felt was really more than he could bear, but as it was smaller, with a few energetic kicks and whisks of his tail he managed to finally dislodge it through the opening, where it fell ignominiously to the earth. The eager eyes of the ever-attendant crow, however, instantly detected it; he flew to the ground, and, turning it over, examined it gravely. It was certainly not edible, but it was exceedingly rare, and, as an old collector of curios, he felt he could not pass it by. He lifted it in his beak, and, with a desperate struggle against the superincumbent weight, regained the branch with his prize. Here, by one of those delicious vagaries of animal nature, he apparently at once discharged his mind of the whole affair, became utterly oblivious of it, allowed it to drop without the least concern, and eventually flew away with an abstracted air, as if he had been another bird entirely. The paper got into a manzanita bush, where it remained suspended until the evening, when, being dislodged by a passing wild-cat on its way to Mulrady's hen-roost, gave that delicately sensitive marauder such a turn that she fled into the adjacent county.

But the troubles of the squirrel were not yet over. On the following day the young man who had accompanied the young woman returned to the trunk, and the squirrel had barely time to make his escape before the impatient visitor approached the opening of the cavity, peered into it, and even passed his hand through its recesses. The delight visible upon his anxious and serious face at the disappearance of the letter, and the apparent proof that it had been called for, showed him to have been its original depositor, and probably awakened a remorseful recollection in the dark bosom of the omnipresent crow, who uttered a conscious-stricken croak from the bough above him. But the young man quickly disappeared again, and the squirrel was once more left in undisputed possession.

A week passed. A weary, anxious interval to Don Cæsar, who had neither seen nor heard from Mamie since their last meeting. Too conscious of his own self-respect to call at the house after the equivocal conduct of Mrs. Mulrady, and too proud to haunt the lanes and approaches in the hope of meeting her daughter, like an ordinary lover, he hid his gloomy thoughts in the monastic shadows of the courtyard at Los Gatos, or found relief in furious riding at night and early morning on the highway. Once or twice the up-stage had been overtaken and passed by a rushing figure as shadowy as a phantom horseman, with only the star-like point of a cigarette to indicate its humanity. It was in one of these fierce recreations that he was obliged to stop in early morning at the blacksmith's shop at Rough-and-Ready, to have a loosened horseshoe replaced, and while waiting picked up a newspaper. Don Cæsar seldom read the papers, but noticing that this was the "Record," he glanced at its columns. A familiar name suddenly flashed out of the dark type like a spark from the anvil. With a brain and heart that seemed to be beating in unison with the blacksmith's sledge, he read as follows: —

"Our distinguished fellow-townsman, Alvin Mulrady, Esq., left town day before yesterday to attend an important meeting of directors of the Red Dog Ditch Company, in San Francisco. Society will regret to hear that Mrs. Mulrady and her beautiful and accomplished daughter, who were expecting to depart for Europe at the end of the month, anticipated the event nearly a fortnight, by taking this opportunity of accompanying Mr. Mulrady as far as San Francisco, on their way to the East. Mrs. and Miss Mulrady intend to visit London, Paris, and Berlin, and will be absent three years. It is possible that Mr. Mulrady may join them later at one or other of those capitals. Considerable disappointment is felt that a more extended leave-taking was not possible, and that, under the circumstances, no opportunity was offered for a 'send off' suitable to the condition of the parties and the esteem in which they are held in Rough-and-Ready."

The paper dropped from his hands. Gone! and without a word! No, that was impossible! There must be some mistake; she had written; the letter had miscarried; she must have sent word to Los Gatos, and the stupid messenger had blundered; she had probably appointed another meeting, or expected him to follow to San Francisco. "The day before yesterday!" It was the morning's paper — she had been gone scarcely two days — it was not too late yet to receive a delayed message by post, by some forgetful hand — by — ah — the tree!

Of course it was in the tree, and he had not been there for a week! Why had he not thought of it before? The fault was his, not hers. Perhaps she had gone away, believing him faithless, or a country boor.

"In the name of the Devil, will you keep me here till eternity!"

The blacksmith stared at him. Don Cæsar suddenly remembered that he was speaking, as he was thinking — in Spanish.

"Ten dollars, my friend, if you have done in five minutes!"

The man laughed. "That's good enough American," he said, beginning to quicken his efforts. Don Cæsar again took up the paper. There was another paragraph that recalled his last interview with Mamie: —

"Mr. Harry Slinn, Jr., the editor of this paper, has just moved into the pioneer house formerly occupied by Alvin Mulrady, Esq., which has already become historic in the annals of the county. Mr. Slinn brings with him his father — H. J. Slinn, Esq. — and his two sisters. Mr. Slinn, Sen., who has been suffering for many years from complete paralysis, we understand is slowly improving; and it is by the advice of his physicians that he has chosen the invigorating air of the foot-hills as a change to the debilitating heat of Sacramento."

The affair had been quickly settled, certainly, reflected Don Cæsar, with a slight chill of jealousy, as he thought of Mamie's interest in the young editor. But the next moment he dismissed it from his mind; all except a dull consciousness that, if she really loved him — Don Cæsar — as he loved her, she could not have assisted in throwing into his society the two young sisters of the editor, whom she expected might be so attractive.

Within the five minutes the horse was ready, and Don Cæsar in the saddle again.

In less than half an hour he was at the wayside boulder. Here he picketed his horse, and took the narrow foot-trail through the hollow. It did not take him long to reach their old trysting-place. With a beating heart he approached the decaying trunk and looked into the cavity. There was no letter there!

A few blackened nuts and some of the dry moss he had put there were lying on the ground at its roots. He could not remember whether they were there when he had last visited the spot. He began to grope in the cavity with both hands. His fingers struck against the sharp angles of a flat paper packet: a thrill of joy ran through them and stopped his beating heart; he drew out the hidden object, and was chilled with disappointment.

It was an ordinary-sized envelope of yellowish-brown paper, bearing, besides the usual government stamp, the official legend of an express company, and showing its age as much by this record of a now obsolete carrying service as by the discoloration of time and atmosphere. Its weight, which was heavier than that of an ordinary letter of the same size and thickness, was evidently due to some loose enclosures, that slightly rustled and could be felt by the fingers, like minute pieces of metal or grains of gravel. It was within Don Cæsar's experience that gold specimens were often sent in that manner. It was in a state of singular preservation, except the address, which, being written in pencil, was scarcely discernible, and even when deciphered appeared to be incoherent and unfinished. The unknown correspondent had written " dear Mary," and then " Mrs. Mary Slinn," with an unintelligible scrawl following for the direction. If Don Cæsar's mind had not been lately preoccupied with the name of the editor, he would hardly have guessed the superscription.

In his cruel disappointment and fully aroused indignation, he at once began to suspect a connection of circumstances which at any other moment he would have thought purely accidental, or perhaps not have considered at all. The cavity in the tree had evidently been used as a secret receptacle for letters before; did Mamie know it at the time, and how did she know it? The apparent age of the letter made it preposterous to suppose that it pointed to any secret correspondence of hers with young Mr. Slinn; and the address was not in her handwriting. Was there any secret previous intimacy between the families? There was but one way in which he could connect this letter with Mamie's faithlessness. It was an infamous, a grotesquely horrible idea, a thought which sprang as much from his inexperience of the world and his habitual suspiciousness of all humor as anything else! It was that the letter was a brutal joke of Slinn's — a joke perhaps concocted by Mamie and himself — a parting insult that should at the last moment proclaim their treachery and his own credulity. Doubtless it contained a declaration of their shame, and the reason why she had fled from him without a word of explanation. And the enclosure, of course, was some significant and degrading illustration. Those Americans were full of those low conceits; it was their national vulgarity.

He held the letter in his angry hand. He could break it open if he wished, and satisfy himself; but it was not addressed to *him*, and the instinct of honor, strong even in his rage, was the instinct of an adversary as well. No; Slinn should open the letter before him. Slinn should explain everything, and answer for it. If it was nothing — a mere accident — it would lead to some general explanation, and perhaps even news of Mamie. But he would arraign Slinn, and at once. He put the letter in his pocket, quickly retraced his steps to his horse, and, putting spurs to the animal, followed the high road to the gate of Mulrady's pioneer cabin.

He remembered it well enough. To a cultivated taste, it was superior to the more pretentious " new house." During the first year of Mulrady's tenancy, the plain square log-cabin had received those additions and attractions which only a tenant can conceive and actual experience suggest; and in this way, the hideous right angles were broken with sheds, " lean-to " extensions, until a certain picturesqueness was given to the irregularity of outline, and a home-like security and companionship to the congregated buildings. It typified the former life of the great capitalist, as the tall new house illustrated the loneliness and isolation that wealth had given him. But the real points of vantage were the years of cultivation and habitation that had warmed and enriched the soil, and evoked the climbing vines and roses that already hid its unpainted boards, rounded its hard outlines, and gave projection and shadow from the pitiless glare of a summer's long sun, or broke the steady beating of the winter rains. It was true that pea and bean poles surrounded it on one side, and the only access to the house was through the cabbage rows that once were the pride and sustenance of the Mulradys. It was this fact, more than any other, that had impelled Mrs. Mulrady to abandon its site; she did not like to read the history of their humble origin reflected in the faces of their visitors as they entered.

Don Cæsar tied his horse to the fence,

and hurriedly approached the house. The door, however, hospitably opened when he was a few paces from it, and when he reached the threshold he found himself unexpectedly in the presence of two pretty girls. They were evidently Slinn's sisters, whom he had neither thought of nor included in the meeting he had prepared. In spite of his preoccupation, he felt himself suddenly embarrassed, not only by the actual distinction of their beauty, but by a kind of likeness that they seemed to bear to Mamie.

"We saw you coming," said the elder, unaffectedly. "You are Don Cæsar Alvarado. My brother has spoken of you."

The words recalled Don Cæsar to himself and a sense of courtesy. He was not here to quarrel with these fair strangers at their first meeting; he must seek Slinn elsewhere, and at another time. The frankness of his reception and the allusion to their brother made it appear impossible that they should be either a party to his disappointment, or even aware of it. His excitement melted away before a certain lazy ease, which the consciousness of their beauty seemed to give them. He was able to put a few courteous inquiries, and, thanks to the paragraph in the " Record," to congratulate them upon their father's improvement.

"Oh, pa is a great deal better in his health, and has picked up even in the last few days, so that he is able to walk round with crutches," said the elder sister. "The air here seems to invigorate him wonderfully."

"And you know, Esther," said the younger, "I think he begins to take more notice of things, especially when he is out-of-doors. He looks around on the scenery, and his eye brightens, as if he knew all about it; and sometimes he knits his brows, and looks down so, as if he was trying to remember."

"You know, I suppose," explained Esther, "that since his seizure his memory has been a blank — that is, three or four years of his life seem to have been dropped out of his recollection."

"It might be a mercy sometimes, Señora,"

said Don Cæsar, with a grave sigh, as he looked at the delicate features before him, which recalled the face of the absent Mamie.

"That's not very complimentary," said the younger girl, laughingly; "for pa didn't recognize us, and only remembered us as little girls."

"Vashti!" interrupted Esther, rebukingly; then, turning to Don Cæsar, she added, "My sister, Vashti, means that father remembers more what happened before he came to California, when we were quite young, than he does of the interval that elapsed. Dr. Duchesne says it's a singular case. He thinks that, with his present progress, he will recover the perfect use of his limbs; though his memory may never come back again."

"Unless — You forget what the doctor told us this morning," interrupted Vashti again, briskly.

"I was going to say it," said Esther, a little curtly. "*Unless* he has another stroke. Then he will either die or recover his mind entirely."

Don Cæsar glanced at the bright faces, a trifle heightened in color by their eager recital and the slight rivalry of narration, and looked grave. He was a little shocked at a certain lack of sympathy and tenderness towards their unhappy parent. They seemed to him not only to have caught that dry, curious toleration of helplessness which characterizes even relationship in its attendance upon chronic suffering and weakness, but to have acquired an unconscious habit of turning it to account. In his present sensitive condition, he even fancied that they flirted mildly over their parent's infirmity.

"My brother Harry has gone to Red Dog," continued Esther; "he'll be right sorry to have missed you. Mrs. Mulrady spoke to him about you; you seem to have been great friends. I s'pose you knew her daughter, Mamie; I hear she is very pretty."

Although Don Cæsar was now satisfied that the Slinns knew nothing of Mamie's singular behavior to him, he felt embarrassed by this conversation. "Miss Mulrady is very pretty," he said, with grave courtesy; "it is a custom of her race. She left suddenly," he added, with affected calmness.

"I reckon she *did* calculate to stay here longer — so her mother said; but the whole thing was settled a week ago. I know my brother was quite surprised to hear from Mr. Mulrady that if we were going to decide about this house we must do it at once; he had an idea himself about moving out of the big one into this when they left."

"Mamie Mulrady had n't much to keep her here, considerin' the money and the good looks she has, I reckon," said Vashti. "She is n't the sort of girl to throw herself away in the wilderness, when she can pick and choose elsewhere. I only wonder she ever come back from Sacramento. They talk about papa Mulrady having *business* at San Francisco, and *that* hurrying them off! Depend upon it, that 'business' was Mamie herself. Her wish is gospel to them. If she 'd wanted to stay and have a farewell party, old Mulrady's business would have been nowhere."

"Ain't you a little rough on Mamie," said Esther, who had been quietly watching the young man's face with her large, languid eyes, "considering that we don't know her, and have n't even the right of friends to criticise?"

"I don't call it rough," returned Vashti, frankly, "for I'd do the same if I were in her shoes — and they 're four-and-a-halves, for Harry told me so. Give me her money and her looks, and you wouldn't catch me hanging round these diggings — goin' to choir meetings Saturdays, church Sundays, and buggy-riding once a month — for society! No — Mamie's head was level — you bet!"

Don Cæsar rose hurriedly. They would present his compliments to their father, and he would endeavor to find their brother at Red Dog. He, alas! had neither father, mother, nor sister, but if they would receive his aunt, the Doña Inez Sepulvida, the next Sunday, when she came from mass, she should be honored and he would be delighted. It required all his self-possession to deliver himself of this formal courtesy before he could take his leave, and on the back of his mustang give way to the rage, disgust, and hatred of everything connected with Mamie that filled his heart. Conscious of his disturbance, but not entirely appreciating their own share in it, the two girls somewhat wickedly prolonged the interview by following him into the garden.

"Well, if you *must* leave now," said Esther, at last, languidly, "it ain't much out of your way to go down through the garden and take a look at pa as you go. He's somewhere down there, near the woods, and we don't like to leave him alone too long. You might pass the time of day with him; see if he's right side up. Vashti and I have got a heap of things to fix here yet; but if anything's wrong with him, you can call us. So-long."

Don Cæsar was about to excuse himself hurriedly; but that sudden and acute perception of all kindred sorrow, which belongs to refined suffering, checked his speech. The loneliness of the helpless old man in this atmosphere of active and youthful selfishness touched him. He bowed assent, and turned aside into one of the long perspectives of bean-poles. The girls watched him until out of sight.

"Well," said Vashti, "don't tell *me*. But if there wasn't something between him and that Mamie Mulrady, I don't know a jilted man when I see him."

"Well, you needn't have let him *see* that you knew it, so that any civility of ours would look as if we were ready to take up with her leavings," responded Esther, astutely, as the girls reëntered the house.

Meantime, the unconscious object of their criticism walked sadly down the old market-garden, whose rude outlines and homely details he once clothed with the poetry of a sensitive man's first love. Well, it was a common cabbage field and potato patch after all. In his disgust he felt conscious of even the loss of that sense of patronage and superiority which had invested his affection for a girl of meaner condition. His self-respect was humiliated with his love. The soil and dirt of those wretched cabbages had clung to him, but not to her. It was she who had gone higher; it was he who was left in the vulgar ruins of his misplaced passion.

He reached the bottom of the garden without observing any sign of the lonely invalid. He looked up and down the cabbage rows, and through the long perspective of pea-vines, without result. There was a newer trail leading from a gap in the pines to the wooded hollow, which undoubtedly intersected the little path that he and Mamie had once followed from the high road. If the old man had taken this trail he had possibly overtasked his strength, and there was the more reason why he should continue his search, and render any assistance if required. There was another idea that occurred to him, which eventually decided him to go on. It was that both these trails led to the decayed sycamore stump, and that the older Slinn might have something to do with the mysterious letter. Quickening his steps through the field, he entered the hollow, and reached the intersecting trail as he expected. To the right it lost itself in the dense woods in the direction of the ominous stump; to the left it descended in nearly a straight line to the highway, now plainly visible, as was equally the boulder on which he had last discovered Mamie sitting with young Slinn. If he was not mistaken, there was a figure sitting there now; it was surely a man. And by that half-bowed, helpless attitude, the object of his search!

It did not take him long to descend the track to the highway and approach the stranger. He was seated with his hands upon his knees, gazing in a vague, absorbed fashion upon the hillside, now crowned with the engine-house and chimney that marked the site of Mulrady's shâft. He started slightly, and looked up, as Don Cæsar paused before him. The young man was surprised to see that the unfortunate man was not as old as he had expected, and that his expression was one of quiet and beatified contentment.

"Your daughters told me you were here," said Don Cæsar, with gentle respect. "I am Cæsar Alvarado, your not very far neighbor; very happy to pay his respects to you as he has to them."

"My daughters?" said the old man, vaguely. "Oh, yes! nice little girls. And my boy Harry. Did you see Harry? Fine little fellow, Harry."

"I am glad to hear that you are better," said Don Cæsar, hastily, "and that the air of our country does you no harm. God benefit you, señor," he added, with a profoundly reverential gesture, dropping unconsciously into the religious habit of his youth, "May he protect you, and bring you back to health and happiness!"

"Happiness?" said Slinn, amazedly. "I am happy — very happy! I have everything I want: good air, good food, good clothes, pretty little children, kind friends " — He smiled benignantly at Don Cæsar. "God is very good to me!"

Indeed, he seemed very happy; and his face, albeit crowned with white hair, unmarked by care and any disturbing impression, had so much of satisfied youth in it that the grave features of his questioner made him appear the elder. Nevertheless, Don Cæsar noticed that his eyes, when withdrawn from him, sought the hillside with the same visionary abstraction.

"It is a fine view, Señor Esslinn," said Don Cæsar.

"It is a beautiful view, sir," said Slinn, turning his happy eyes upon him for a moment, only to rest them again on the green slope opposite.

"Beyond that hill which you are looking at — not far, Señor Esslinn — I live. You shall come and see me there — you and your family."

"You — you — live there?" stammered the invalid, with a troubled expression — the first and only change to the complete happiness that had hitherto suffused his face. "You — and your name is — is Ma —"

"Alvarado," said Don Cæsar, gently. "Cæsar Alvarado."

"You said Masters," said the old man, with sudden querulousness.

"No, good friend. I said Alvarado," returned Don Cæsar, gravely.

"If you did n't say Masters, how could *I* say it? I don't know any Masters."

Don Cæsar was silent. In another moment the happy tranquillity returned to Slinn's face; and Don Cæsar continued: —

"It is not a long walk over the hill, though it is far by the road. When you are better you shall try it. Yonder little trail leads to the top of the hill, and then" —

He stopped, for the invalid's face had again assumed its troubled expression. Partly to change his thoughts, and partly for some inexplicable idea that had suddenly seized him, Don Cæsar continued: —

"There is a strange old stump near the trail, and in it a hole. In the hole I found this letter." He stopped again — this time in alarm. Slinn had staggered to his feet with ashen and distorted features, and was glancing at the letter which Don Cæsar had drawn from his pocket. The muscles of his throat swelled as if he was swallowing; his lips moved, but no sound issued from them.

At last, with a convulsive effort, he regained a disjointed speech, in a voice scarcely audible.

"My letter! my letter! It's mine! Give it me! It's my fortune — all mine! In the tunnel — hill! Masters stole it — stole my fortune! Stole it all! See, see!"

He seized the letter from Don Cæsar with trembling hands, and tore it open forcibly: a few dull yellow grains fell from it heavily, like shot, to the ground.

"See, it's true! My letter! My gold! My strike! My — my — my God!"

A tremor passed over his face. The hand that held the letter suddenly dropped sheer and heavy as the gold had fallen. The whole side of his face and body nearest Don Cæsar seemed to drop and sink into itself as suddenly. At the same moment, and without a word, he slipped through Don Cæsar's outstretched hands to the ground. Don Cæsar bent quickly over him, but not longer than to satisfy himself that he lived and breathed, although helpless. He then caught up the fallen letter, and, glancing over it with flashing eyes, thrust it and the few specimens in his pocket. He then sprang to his feet, so transformed with energy and intelligence that he seemed to have added the lost vitality of the man before him to his own. He glanced quickly up and down the highway. Every moment to him was precious now; but he could not leave the stricken man in the dust of the road; nor could he carry him to the house; nor, having alarmed his daughters, could he abandon his helplessness to their feeble arms. He remembered that his horse was still tied to the garden fence. He would fetch it, and carry the unfortunate man across the saddle to the gate. He lifted him with difficulty to the boulder, and ran rapidly up the road in the direction of his tethered steed. He had not proceeded far when he heard the noise of wheels behind him. It was the up-stage coming furiously along. He would have called to the driver for assistance, but even through that fast-sweeping cloud of dust and motion he could see that the man was utterly oblivious of anything but the speed of his rushing chariot, and had even risen in his box to lash the infuriated and frightened animals forward.

An hour later, when the coach drew up at the Red Dog Hotel, the driver descended from the box, white, but taciturn. When he had swallowed a glass of whiskey at a single gulp, he turned to the astonished express agent, who had followed him in.

"One of two things, Jim, hez got to happen," he said, huskily. "Either that there rock hez got to get off the road, or *I* have. I 've seed *him* on it agin!"

CHAPTER IV.

No further particulars of the invalid's second attack were known than those furnished by Don Cæsar's brief statement, that he had found him lying insensible on the boulder. This seemed perfectly consistent with the theory of Dr. Duchesne; and as the young Spaniard left Los Gatos the next day, he escaped not only the active reporter of the "Record," but the perusal of a grateful paragraph in the next day's paper recording his prompt kindness and courtesy. Dr. Duchesne's prognosis, however, seemed at fault; the elder Slinn did not succumb to this second stroke, nor did he recover his reason. He apparently only relapsed into his former physical weakness, losing the little ground he had gained during the last month, and exhibiting no change in his mental condition, unless the fact that he remembered nothing of his seizure and the presence of Don Cæsar could be considered as favorable. Dr. Duchesne's gravity seemed to give that significance to this symptom, and his cross-questioning of the patient was characterized by more than his usual curtness.

"You are sure you don't remember walking in the garden before you were ill?" he said. "Come, think again. You must remember that." The old man's eyes wandered restlessly around the room, but he answered by a negative shake of his head. "And you don't remember sitting down on a stone by the road?"

The old man kept his eyes resolutely fixed on the bed-clothes before him. "No!" he said, with a certain sharp decision that was new to him.

The doctor's eye brightened. "All right, old man; then don't."

On his way out he took the eldest Miss Slinn aside. "He'll do," he said, grimly: "he's beginning to lie."

"Why, he only said he did n't remember," responded Esther.

"That was because he didn't want to remember," said the doctor, authoritatively. "The brain is acting on some impression that is either painful and unpleasant, or so vague that he can't formulate it; he is conscious of it, and won't attempt it yet. It's a heap better than his old self-satisfied incoherency."

A few days later, when the fact of Slinn's identification with the paralytic of three years ago by the stage-driver became generally known, the doctor came in quite jubilant.

"It's all plain now," he said, decidedly. "That second stroke was caused by the nervous shock of his coming suddenly upon the very spot where he had the first one. It proved that his brain still retained old impressions, but as this first act of his memory was a painful one, the strain was too great. It was mighty unlucky; but it was a good sign."

"And you think, then"—hesitated Harry Slinn.

"I think," said Dr. Duchesne, "that this

activity still exists, and the proof of it, as I said before, is that he is trying now to forget it, and avoid thinking of it. You will find that he will fight shy of any allusion to it, and will be cunning enough to dodge it every time."

He certainly did. Whether the doctor's hypothesis was fairly based or not, it was a fact that, when he was first taken out to drive with his watchful physician, he apparently took no notice of the boulder — which still remained on the roadside, thanks to the later practical explanation of the stage-driver's vision — and curtly refused to talk about it. But, more significant to Duchesne, and perhaps more perplexing, was a certain morose abstraction, which took the place of his former vacuity of contentment, and an intolerance of his attendants, which supplanted his old habitual trustfulness to their care, that had been varied only by the occasional querulousness of an invalid. His daughters sometimes found him regarding them with an attention little short of suspicion, and even his son detected a half-suppressed aversion in his interviews with him.

Referring this among themselves to his unfortunate malady, his children, perhaps, justified this estrangement by paying very little attention to it. They were more pleasantly occupied. The two girls succeeded to the position held by Mamie Mulrady in the society of the neighborhood, and divided the attentions of Rough-and-Ready. The young editor of the "Record" had really achieved, through his supposed intimacy with the Mulradys, the good fortune he had jestingly prophesied. The disappearance of Don Cæsar was regarded as a virtual abandonment of the field to his rival: and the general opinion was that he was engaged to the millionaire's daughter on a certain probation of work and influence in his prospective father-in-law's interests. He became successful in one or two speculations, the magic of the lucky Mulrady's name befriending him. In the superstition of the mining community, much of this luck was due to his having secured the old cabin.

"To think," remarked one of the augurs of Red Dog, French Pete, a polyglot jester, "that while every d——d fool went to taking up claims where the gold had already been found, no one thought of stepping into the old man's old *choux* in the cabbage-garden!" Any doubt, however, of the alliance of the families was dissipated by the intimacy that sprang up between the elder Slinn and the millionaire, after the latter's return from San Francisco.

It began in a strange kind of pity for the physical weakness of the man, which enlisted the sympathies of Mulrady, whose great strength had never been deteriorated by the luxuries of wealth, and who was still able to set his workmen an example of hard labor; it was sustained by a singular and superstitious reverence for his mental condition, which, to the paternal Mulrady, seemed to possess that spiritual quality with which popular ignorance invests demented people.

"Then you mean to say that during these three years the vein o' your mind, so to speak, was a lost lead, and sorter dropped out o' sight or follerin'?" queried Mulrady, with infinite seriousness.

"Yes," returned Slinn, with less impatience than he usually showed to questions.

"And durin' that time, when you was dried up and waitin' for rain, I reckon you kinder had visions?"

A cloud passed over Slinn's face.

"Of course, of course!" said Mulrady, a little frightened at his tenacity in questioning the oracle. "Nat'rally, this was private, and not to be talked about. I meant, you had plenty of room for 'em without crowdin'; you kin tell me some day when you're better, and kin sorter select what's points and what ain't."

"Perhaps I may some day," said the invalid, gloomily, glancing in the direction of his preoccupied daughters; "when we're alone."

When his physical strength had improved, and his left arm and side had regained a feeble but slowly gathering vitality, Alvin Mulrady one day surprised the family by bringing the convalescent a pile of letters and accounts, and spreading them on a board before Slinn's invalid chair, with the suggestion that he should look over, arrange, and docket them. The idea seemed preposterous, until it was found that the old man was actually able to perform this service, and exhibited a degree of intellectual activity and capacity for this kind of work that was unsuspected. Dr. Duchesne was delighted, and divided with admiration between his patient's progress and the millionaire's sagacity. "And there are envious people," said the enthusiastic doctor, "who believe that a man like him, who could conceive of such a plan for occupying a weak intellect without taxing its memory or judgment, is merely a lucky fool! Look here. May be it did n't require much brains to stumble on a gold mine, and it is a gift of Providence. But, in my experience, Providence don't go round buyin' up d——d fools, or investin' in dead beats."

When Mr. Slinn, finally, with the aid of crutches, was able to hobble every day to the imposing counting-house and office of Mr.

Mulrady, which now occupied the lower part of the new house, and contained some of its gorgeous furniture, he was installed at a rosewood desk behind Mr. Mulrady's chair, as his confidential clerk and private secretary. The astonishment of Red Dog and Rough-and-Ready at this singular innovation knew no bounds; but the boldness and novelty of the idea carried everything before it. Judge Butts, the oracle of Rough-and-Ready, delivered its decision: "He's got a man who's physically incapable of running off with his money, and has no memory to run off with his ideas. How could he do better?" Even his own son, Harry, coming upon his father thus installed, was for a moment struck with a certain filial respect, and for a day or two patronized him.

In this capacity Slinn became the confidant not only of Mulrady's business secrets, but of his domestic affairs. He knew that young Mulrady, from a freckle-faced, slow country boy had developed into a freckle-faced fast city man, with coarse habits of drink and gambling. It was through the old man's hands that extravagant bills and shameful claims passed on their way to be cashed by Mulrady; it was he that at last laid before the father one day his signature perfectly forged by the son.

"Your eyes are not ez good ez mine, you know, Slinn," said Mulrady, gravely. "It's all right. I sometimes make my y's like that. I'd clean forgot to cash that check. You must not think you've got the monoply of disremembering," he added, with a faint laugh.

Equally through Slinn's hands passed the record of the lavish expenditure of Mrs. Mulrady and the fair Mamie, as well as the chronicle of their movements and fashionable triumphs. As Mulrady had already noticed that Slinn had no confidence with his own family, he did not try to withhold from them these domestic details, possibly as an offset to the dreary catalogue of his son's misdeeds, but more often in the hope of gaining from the taciturn old man some comment that might satisfy his innocent vanity as father and husband, and perhaps dissipate some doubts that were haunting him.

"Twelve hundred dollars looks to be a good figger for a dress, ain't it? But Malviny knows, I reckon, what ought to be worn at the Tooilleries, and she don't want our Mamie to take a back seat before them furrin' princesses and gran' dukes. It's a slap-up affair, I kalkilate. Let's see. I disremember whether it's an emperor or a king that's rulin' over thar now. It must be suthin' first class and A 1, for Malviny ain't the woman to throw away twelve hundred dollars on any of them small-potato despots! She says Mamie speaks French already like them French Petes. I don't quite make out what she means here. She met Don Cæsar in Paris, and she says, 'I think Mamie is nearly off with Don Cæsar, who has followed her here. I don't care about her dropping him *too* suddenly; the reason I'll tell you hereafter. I think the man might be a dangerous enemy.' Now, what do you make of this? I allus thought Mamie rather cottoned to him, and it was the old woman who fought shy, thinkin' Mamie would do better. Now, I am agreeable that my gal should marry any one she likes, whether it's a dook or a poor man, as long as he's on the square. I was ready to take Don Cæsar; but now things seem to have shifted round. As to Don Cæsar's being a dangerous enemy if Mamie won't have him, that's a little too high and mighty for me, and I wonder the old woman don't make him climb down. What do you think?"

"Who is Don Cæsar?" asked Slinn.

"The man what picked you up that day. I mean," continued Mulrady, seeing the marks of evident ignorance on the old man's face, — "I mean a sort of grave, genteel chap, suthin' between a parson and a circus-rider. You might have seen him round the house talkin' to your gals."

But Slinn's entire forgetfulness of Don Cæsar was evidently unfeigned. Whatever sudden accession of memory he had at the time of his attack, the incident that caused it had no part in his recollection. With the exception of these rare intervals of domestic confidences with his crippled private secretary, Mulrady gave himself up to money-getting. Without any especial faculty for it — an easy prey often to unscrupulous financiers — his unfailing luck, however, carried him safely through, until his very mistakes seemed to be simply insignificant means to a large significant end and a part of his original plan. He sank another shaft, at a great expense, with a view to following the lead he had formerly found, against the opinions of the best mining engineers, and struck the artesian spring he did *not* find at that time, with a volume of water that enabled him not only to work his own mine, but to furnish supplies to his less fortunate neighbors at a vast profit. A league of tangled forest and cañon behind Rough-and-Ready, for which he had paid Don Ramon's heirs an extravagant price in the presumption that it was auriferous, furnished the most accessible timber to build the town, at prices which amply remunerated him. The practical schemes of experienced men, the wildest visions of daring dreams delayed or abortive for want of capital, eventually fell into his hands. Men sneered at his methods, but bought his shares. Some who affected to regard him simply as a man of money were content to get only his name to any enterprise. Courted by his superiors, quoted by his equals, and admired by his inferiors, he bore his elevation equally without ostentation or dignity. Bidden to banquets, and forced by his position as director or president into the usual gastronomic feats of that civilization and period, he partook of simple food, and continued his old habit of taking a cup of coffee with milk and sugar at dinner. Without professing temperance, he drank sparingly in a community where alcoholic stimulation was a custom. With neither refinement nor an extended vocabulary, he was seldom profane, and never indelicate. With nothing of the Puritan in his manner or conversation, he seemed to be as strange to the vices of civilization as he was to its virtues. That such a man should offer little to and receive little from the companionship of women of any kind was a foregone conclusion. Without the dignity of solitude, he was pathetically alone.

Meantime, the days passed; the first six months of his opulence were drawing to a close, and in that interval he had more than doubled the amount of his discovered fortune. The rainy season set in early. Although it dissipated the clouds of dust under which Nature and Art seemed to be slowly disappearing, it brought little beauty to the landscape at first, and only appeared to lay bare the crudenesses of civilization. The unpainted wooden buildings of Rough-and-Ready, soaked and dripping with rain, took upon themselves a sleek and shining ugliness, as of second-hand garments; the absence of cornices or projections to break the monotony of the long straight lines of downpour made the town appear as if it had been recently submerged, every vestige of ornamentation swept away, and only the bare outlines left. Mud was everywhere; the outer soil seemed to have risen and invaded the houses even to their most secret recesses, as if outraged Nature was trying to revenge herself. Mud was brought into the saloons and bar-rooms and express offices, on boots, on clothes, on baggage, and sometimes appeared mysteriously in splashes of red color on the walls, without visible conveyance. The dust of six months, closely packed in cornice and carving, yielded under the steady rain a thin yellow paint, that dropped on wayfarers or unexpectedly oozed out of ceilings and walls on the wretched inhabitants within. The outskirts of Rough-and-Ready and the dried hills round Los Gatos did not appear to fare much better; the new vegetation had not yet made much headway against the dead grasses of the summer; the pines in the hollow wept lugubriously into a small rivulet that had sprung suddenly into life near the old trail; everywhere was the sound of dropping, splashing, gurgling, or rushing waters.

More hideous than ever, the new Mulrady house lifted itself against the leaden sky, and stared with all its large-framed, shutterless windows blankly on the prospect, until they seemed to the wayfarer to become mere mirrors set in the walls, reflecting only the watery landscape, and unable to give the least indication of light or heat within. Nevertheless, there was a fire in Mulrady's private office that December afternoon, of a smoky, intermittent variety, that sufficed more to record the defects of hasty architecture than to comfort the millionaire and his private secretary, who had lingered after the early withdrawal of the clerks. For the next day was Christmas, and, out of deference to the near approach of this festivity, a half-holiday had been given to the employés. "They 'll want, some of them, to spend their money before to-morrow; and others would like to be able to rise up comfortably drunk Christmas morning," the superintendent had suggested. Mr. Mulrady had just signed a number of checks indicating his largess to those devoted adherents with the same unostentatious, undemonstrative, matter-of-fact manner that distinguished his ordinary business. The men had received it with something of the same manner. A half-humorous "Thank you, sir" — as if to show that, with their patron, they tolerated this deference to a popular custom, but were a little ashamed of giving way to it — expressed their gratitude and their independence.

"I reckon that the old lady and Mamie are having a high old time in some of them gilded pallises in St. Petersburg or Berlin about this time. Them diamonds that I ordered at Tiffany ought to have reached 'em about now, so that Mamie could cut a swell at Christmas with her war-paint. I suppose it's the style to give presents in furrin' countries ez it is here, and I allowed to the old lady that whatever she orders in that way she is to do in Californy style — no dollar-jewelry and galvanized-watches business. If she wants to make a present to any of them nobles ez has been purlite to her, it's got to be something that Rough-and-Ready ain't ashamed of. I showed you that pin Mamie bought me in Paris, did n't I? It's just come for my Christmas present. No! I reckon I put it in the safe, for them kind o' things don't suit my style: but s'pose I orter sport it to-morrow. It was mighty thoughtful in Mamie, and it must cost a lump; it's got no slouch of a pearl in it. I wonder what Mamie gave for it?"

"You can easily tell; the bill is here. You paid it yesterday," said Slinn. There was no satire in the man's voice, nor was there the least perception of irony in Mulrady's manner, as he returned quietly, —

"That's so; it was suthin' like a thousand francs; but French money, when you pan it out as dollars and cents, don't make so much, after all." There was a few moments' silence, when he continued, in the same tone of voice, "Talkin' o' them things, Slinn, I've got suthin' for you." He stopped suddenly. Ever watchful of any undue excitement in the invalid, he had noticed a slight flush of disturbance pass over his face, and continued carelessly, "But we'll talk it over to-morrow; a day or two don't make much difference to you and me in such things, you know. P'raps I'll drop in and see you. We'll be shut up here."

"Then you're going out somewhere?" asked Slinn, mechanically.

"No," said Mulrady, hesitatingly. It had suddenly occurred to him that he had nowhere to go, if he wanted to, and he continued, half in explanation, "I ain't reckoned much on Christmas, myself. Abner's at the Springs; it would n't pay him to come here for a day — even if there was anybody here he cared to see. I reckon I'll hang round the shanty, and look after things generally. I have n't been over the house upstairs to put things to rights since the folks left. But *you* need n't come here, you know."

He helped the old man to rise, assisted him in putting on his overcoat, and then handed him the cane which had lately replaced his crutches.

"Good-by, old man! You must n't trouble yourself to say 'Merry Christmas' now, but wait until you see me again. Take care of yourself."

He slapped him lightly on the shoulder, and went back into his private office. He worked for some time at his desk, and then laid his pen aside, put away his papers methodically, placing a large envelope on his private secretary's vacant table. He then opened the office door and ascended the staircase. He stopped on the first landing to listen to the sound of rain on the glass skylight, that seemed to echo through the empty hall like the gloomy roll of a drum. It was evident that the searching water had found out the secret sins of the house's construction, for there were great fissures of discoloration in the white and gold paper in the corners of the wall. There was a strange odor of the dank forest in the mirrored drawing-room, as if the rain had brought out the sap again from the unseasoned timbers; the blue and white satin furniture looked cold, and the marble mantels and centre tables had taken upon themselves the clamminess of tombstones. Mr. Mulrady, who had always retained his old farmer-like habit of taking off his coat with his hat on entering his own house, and appearing in his shirt-sleeves, to indicate domestic ease and security, was obliged to replace it, on account of the chill. He had never felt at home in this room. Its strangeness had lately been heightened by Mrs. Mulrady's purchase of a family portrait of some one she did n't know, but who, she had alleged, resembled her "Uncle Bob," which hung on the wall beside some paintings in massive frames. Mr. Mulrady cast a hurried glance at the portrait that, on the strength of a high coat-collar and high top curl — both rolled with equal precision and singular sameness of color — had always glared at Mulrady as if *he* was the intruder; and, passing through his wife's gorgeous bedroom, entered the little dressing-room, where he still slept on the smallest of cots, with hastily improvised surroundings, as if he was a bailiff in "possession." He did n't linger here long, but, taking a key from a drawer, continued up the staircase, to the ominous funeral marches of the beating rain on the skylight, and paused on the landing to glance into his son's and daughter's bedrooms, duplicates of the *bizarre* extravagance below. If he were seeking some characteristic traces of his absent family, they certainly were not here in the painted and still damp blazoning of their later successes. He ascended another staircase, and, passing to the wing of the house, paused before a small door, which was locked. Already the ostentatious decorations of wall and passages were left behind, and the plain lath-and-plaster partition of the attic lay before him. He unlocked the door, and threw it open.

CHAPTER V.

THE apartment he entered was really only a lumber-room or loft over the wing of the house, which had been left bare and unfinished, and which revealed in its meagre skeleton of beams and joints the hollow sham of the whole structure. But in more violent contrast to the fresher glories of the other part of the house were its contents, which were the heterogeneous collection of old furniture, old luggage, and cast-off clothing, left over from the past life in the old cabin. It was a much plainer record of the simple beginnings of the family than Mrs. Mulrady cared to have remain in evidence, and for that reason it had been relegated to the hidden recesses of the new house, in the hope that it might absorb or digest it. There were old cribs, in which the infant limbs of Mamie and Abner had been tucked up; old looking-glasses, that had reflected their shining, soapy faces, and Mamie's best chip Sunday hat; an old sewing-machine, that had been worn out in active service; old patchwork quilts; an old accordion, to whose long drawn inspirations Mamie had sung hymns; old pictures, books, and old toys. There were one or two old chromos, and, stuck in an old frame, a colored print from the " Illustrated London News " of a Christmas gathering in an old English country house. He stopped and picked up this print, which he had often seen before, gazing at it with a new and singular interest. He wondered if Mamie had seen anything of this kind in England, and why could n't he have had something like it here, in their own fine house, with themselves and a few friends? He remembered a past Christmas, when he had bought Mamie that now headless doll with the few coins that were left him after buying their frugal Christmas dinner. There was an old spotted hobby-horse that another Christmas had brought to Abner — Abner, who would be driving a fast trotter to-morrow at the Springs! How everything had changed!

How they all had got up in the world, and how far beyond this kind of thing — and yet — yet it would have been rather comfortable to have all been together again here. Would *they* have been more comfortable? No! Yet then he might have had something to do, and been less lonely to-morrow. What of that? He *had* something to do: to look after this immense fortune. What more could a man want, or should he want? It was rather mean in him, able to give his wife and children everything they wanted, to be wanting anything more. He laid down the print gently, after dusting its glass and frame with his silk handkerchief, and slowly left the room.

The drum-beat of the rain followed him down the staircase, but he shut it out with his other thoughts, when he again closed the door of his office. He sat diligently to work by the declining winter light, until he was interrupted by the entrance of his Chinese waiter to tell him that supper — which was the meal that Mulrady religiously adhered to in place of the late dinner of civilization

— was ready in the dining-room. Mulrady mechanically obeyed the summons; but on entering the room, the oasis of a few plates in a desert of white table-cloth which awaited him made him hesitate. In its best aspect, the high dark Gothic mahogany ecclesiastical sideboard and chairs of this room, which looked like the appointments of a mortuary chapel, were not exhilarating; and to-day, in the light of the rain-filmed windows and the feeble rays of a lamp half obscured by the dark, shining walls, it was most depressing.

"You kin take up supper into my office," said Mulrady, with a sudden inspiration. "I'll eat it there."

He ate it there, with his usual healthy appetite, which did not require even the stimulation of company. He had just finished, when his Irish cook — the one female servant of the house — came to ask permission to be absent that evening and the next day.

"I suppose the likes of your honor won't be at home on the Christmas Day? And it's me cousins from the old counthry at Rough-and-Ready that are invitin' me."

"Why don't you ask them over here?" said Mulrady, with another vague inspiration. "I'll stand treat."

"Lord preserve you for a jinerous gintleman! But it's the likes of them and myself that would n't be at home here on such a day."

There was so much truth in this that Mulrady checked a sigh as he gave the required permission, without saying that he had intended to remain. He could cook his own breakfast: he had done it before; and it would be something to occupy him. As to his dinner, perhaps he could go to the hotel at Rough-and-Ready. He worked on until the night had well advanced. Then, overcome with a certain restlessness that disturbed him, he was forced to put his books and papers away. It had begun to blow in fitful gusts, and occasionally the rain was driven softly across the panes like the passing of childish fingers. This disturbed him more than the monotony of silence, for he was not a nervous man. He seldom read a book, and the county paper furnished him only the financial and mercantile news which was part of his business. He knew he could not sleep, if he went to bed. At last he rose, opened the window, and looked out from pure idleness of occupation. A splash of wheels in the distant muddy road and fragments of a drunken song showed signs of an early wandering reveller. There were no lights to be seen at the closed works; a profound darkness encompassed the house, as if the distant pines in the hollow had moved up and round it. The silence was broken now only by the occasional sighing of wind and rain. It was not an inviting night for a perfunctory walk; but an idea struck him — he would call upon the Slinns, and anticipate his next day's visit! They would probably have company, and be glad to see him: he could tell the girls of Mamie and her success. That he had not thought of this before was a proof of his usual self-contained isolation; that he thought of it now was an equal proof that he was becoming at last accessible to loneliness. He was angry with himself for what seemed to him a selfish weakness.

He returned to his office, and, putting the envelope that had been lying on Slinn's desk in his pocket, threw a *serape* over his shoulders, and locked the front door of the house behind him. It was well that the way was a familiar one to him, and that his feet instinctively found the trail, for the night was very dark. At times he was warned only by the gurgling of water of little rivulets that descended the hill and crossed his path. Without the slightest fear, and with neither imagination nor sensitiveness, he recalled how, the winter before, one of Don Cæsar's vaqueros, crossing this hill at night, had fallen down the chasm of a landslip caused by the rain, and was found the next morning with his neck broken in the gully. Don Cæsar had to take care of the man's family. Suppose such an accident should happen to him? Well, he had made his will. His wife and children would be provided for, and the work of the mine would go on all the same; he had arranged for that. Would anybody miss him? Would his wife, or his son, or his daughter? No. He felt such a sudden and overwhelming conviction of the truth of this, that he stopped as suddenly as if the chasm had opened before him. No! It was the truth. If he were to disappear forever in the darkness of the Christmas night, there was none to feel his loss. His wife would take care of Mamie; his son would take care of himself, as he had before — relieved of even the scant paternal authority he rebelled against. A more imaginative man than Mulrady would have combated or have followed out this idea, and then dismissed it; to the millionaire's matter-of-fact mind it was a deduction that, having once presented itself to his perception, was already a recognized fact. For the first time in his life he felt a sudden instinct of something like aversion towards his family, a feeling that even his son's dissipation and criminality had never provoked. He hurried on angrily through the darkness.

It was very strange; the old house should be almost before him now, across the hollow, yet there were no indications of light! It was not until he actually reached the garden-fence, and the black bulk of shadow rose out against the sky, that he saw a faint ray of light from one of the lean-to windows. He went to the front door and knocked. After waiting in vain for a reply, he knocked again. The second knock proving equally futile, he tried the door; it was unlocked, and, pushing it open, he walked in. The narrow passage was quite dark, but from his knowledge of the house he knew the "lean-to" was next to the kitchen, and, passing through the dining-room into it, he opened the door of the little room from which the light proceeded. It came from a single candle on a small table, and beside it, with his eyes moodily fixed on the dying embers of the fire, sat old Slinn. There was no other light nor another human being in the whole house.

For the instant Mulrady, forgetting his own feelings in the mute picture of the utter desolation of the helpless man, remained speechless on the threshold. Then, recalling himself, he stepped forward and laid his hand gayly on the bowed shoulders.

"Rouse up out o' this, old man! Come! this won't do. Look! I've run over here in the rain, jist to have a sociable time with you all."

"I knew it," said the old man, without looking up; "I knew you'd come."

"You knew I'd come?" echoed Mulrady, with an uneasy return of the strange feeling of awe with which he regarded Slinn's abstraction.

"Yes; you were alone — like myself — all alone!"

"Then, why in thunder did n't you open the door or sing out just now?" he said, with an affected *brusquerie* to cover his uneasiness. "Where's your daughters?"

"Gone to Rough-and-Ready to a party."

"And your son?"

"He never comes here when he can amuse himself elsewhere."

"Your children might have stayed home on Christmas Eve."

"So might yours."

He did n't say this impatiently, but with a certain abstracted conviction far beyond any suggestion of its being a retort. Mulrady did not appear to notice it.

"Well, I don't see why us old folks can't enjoy ourselves without them," said Mulrady, with affected cheerfulness. "Let's have a good time, you and me. Let's see — you haven't any one you can send to my house, hev you?"

"They took the servant with them," said Slinn, briefly. "There is no one here."

"All right," said the millionaire, briskly. "I'll go myself. Do you think you could manage to light up a little more, and build a fire in the kitchen while I'm gone? It used to be mighty comfortable in the old times."

He helped the old man to rise from his chair, and seemed to have infused into him some of his own energy. He then added, "Now, don't you get yourself down again into that chair until I come back," and darted out into the night once more.

In a quarter of an hour he returned with a bag on his broad shoulders, which one of his porters would have shrunk from lifting, and laid it before the blazing hearth of the now-lighted kitchen. "It's something the old woman got for her party, that did n't come off," he said, apologetically. "I reckon we can pick out enough for a spread. That darned Chinaman would n't come with me," he added, with a laugh, "because, he said, he 'd knocked off work 'allee same, Mellican man!' Look here, Slinn," he said, with a sudden decisiveness, "my pay-roll of the men around here don't run short of a hundred and fifty dollars a day, and yet I could n't get a hand to help me bring this truck over for my Christmas dinner."

"Of course," said Slinn, gloomily.

"Of course; so it oughter be," returned Mulrady, shortly. "Why, it's only their one day out of 364; and I can have 363 days off, as I am their boss. I don't mind a man's being independent," he continued, taking off his coat and beginning to unpack his sack — a common "gunny bag" — used for potatoes. "We're independent ourselves, ain't we, Slinn?"

His good spirits, which had been at first

labored and affected, had become natural. Slinn, looking at his brightened eye and fresher color, could not help thinking he was more like his own real self at this moment than in his counting-house and offices — with all his simplicity as a capitalist. A less abstracted and more observant critic than Slinn would have seen in this patient aptitude for real work, and the recognition of the force of petty detail, the dominance of the old market-gardener in his former humble, as well as his later more ambitious, successes.

"Heaven keep us from being dependent upon our children!" said Slinn, darkly.

"Let the young ones alone to-night; we can get along without them, as they can without us," said Mulrady, with a slight twinge as he thought of his reflections on the hillside. "But look here, there's some champagne and them sweet cordials that women like; there's jellies and such like stuff, about as good as they make 'em, I reckon; and preserves, and tongues, and spiced beef — take your pick! Stop, let's spread them out." He dragged the table to the middle of the floor, and piled the provisions upon it. They certainly were not deficient in quality or quantity. "Now, Slinn, wade in."

"I don't feel hungry," said the invalid, who had lapsed again into a chair before the fire.

"No more do I," said Mulrady; "but I reckon it's the right thing to do about this time. Some folks think they can't be happy without they're getting outside o' suthin', and my directors down at 'Frisco can't do any business without a dinner. Take some champagne, to begin with."

He opened a bottle, and filled two tumblers. "It's past twelve o'clock, old man, so here's a merry Christmas to you, and both of us ez is here. And here's another to our families — ez is n't."

They both drank their wine stolidly. The rain beat against the windows sharply, but without the hollow echoes of the house on the hill. "I must write to the old woman and Mamie, and say that you and me had a high old time on Christmas Eve."

"By ourselves," added the invalid.

Mr. Mulrady coughed. "Nat'rally — by ourselves. And her provisions," he added, with a laugh. "We're really beholden to *her* for 'em. If she had n't thought of having them "—

"For somebody else, you would n't have had them — would you?" said Slinn, slowly, gazing at the fire.

"No," said Mulrady, dubiously. After a pause he began more vivaciously, and as if to shake off some disagreeable thought that was impressing him, "But I must n't forget to give you *your* Christmas, old man, and I 've got it right here with me." He took the folded envelope from his pocket, and, holding it in his hand with his elbow on the table, continued, "I don't mind telling you what idea I had in giving you what I 'm goin' to give you now. I 've been thinking about it for a day or two. A man like you don't want money — you would n't spend it. A man like you don't want stocks or fancy investments, for you could n't look after them. A man like you don't want diamonds and jewellery, nor a gold-headed cane, when it's got to be used as a crutch. No, sir. What you want is suthin' that won't run away from you; that is always there before you and won't wear out, and will last after you're gone. That's land! And if it wasn't that I have sworn never to sell or give away this house and that garden, if it wasn't that I've held out agin the old woman and Mamie on that point, you should have *this* house and *that* garden. But, mebbee, for the same reason that I've told you, I want that land to keep for myself. But I've selected four acres of the hill this side of my shaft, and here's the deed of it. As soon as you're ready, I'll put you up a house as big as this — that shall be yours, with the land, as long as you live, old man; and after that your children's."

"No; not theirs!" broke in the old man, passionately. "Never!"

Mulrady recoiled for an instant in alarm at the sudden and unexpected vehemence of his manner. "Go slow, old man; go slow," he said, soothingly. "Of course, you'll do with your own as you like." Then, as if changing the subject, he went on cheerfully: "Perhaps you'll wonder why I picked out that spot on the hillside. Well, first, because I reserved it after my strike in case the lead should run that way, but it didn't. Next, because when you first came here you seemed to like the prospect. You used to sit there looking at it, as if it reminded you of something. You never said it did. They say you was sitting on that boulder there when you had that last attack, you know; but," he added, gently, "you've forgotten all about it."

"I have forgotten nothing," said Slinn, rising, with a choking voice. "I wish to God I had; I wish to God I could!"

He was on his feet now, supporting himself by the table. The subtle generous liquor he had drunk had evidently shaken his self-control, and burst those voluntary bonds he had put upon himself for the last six months; the insidious stimulant had also put a strange vigor into his blood and nerves. His face was flushed, but not distorted; his eyes were brilliant, but not fixed; he looked as he might have looked to Masters in his strength three years before on that very hillside.

"Listen to me, Alvin Mulrady," he said, leaning over him with burning eyes. "Listen, while I have brain to think and strength to utter, why I have learnt to distrust, fear, and hate them! You think you know my story. Well, hear the truth from *me* to-night, Alvin Mulrady, and do not wonder if I have cause."

He stopped, and, with pathetic inefficiency, passed the fingers and inward-turned thumb of his paralyzed hand across his mouth, as if to calm himself. "Three years ago I was a miner, but not a miner like you! I had experience, I had scientific knowledge, I had a theory, and the patience and energy to carry it out. I selected a spot that had all the indications, made a tunnel, and, without aid, counsel, or assistance of any kind, worked it for six months, without rest or cessation, and with scarcely food enough to sustain my body. Well, I made a strike; not like you

Mulrady, not a blunder of good luck, a fool's fortune — there, I don't blame you for it — but in perfect demonstration of my theory, the reward of my labor. It was no pocket, but a vein, a lead, that I had regularly hunted down and found — a fortune!

"I never knew how hard I had worked until that morning; I never knew what privations I had undergone until that moment of my success, when I found I could scarcely think or move! I staggered out into the open air. The only human soul near me was a disappointed prospector, a man named Masters, who had a tunnel not far away. I managed to conceal from him my good fortune and my feeble state, for I was suspicious of him — of any one; and as he was going away that day I thought I could keep my secret until he was gone. I was dizzy and confused, but I remember that I managed to write a letter to my wife, telling her of my good fortune, and begging her to come to me; and I remember that I saw Masters go. I don't remember anything else. They picked me up on the road, near that boulder, as you know."

"I know," said Mulrady, with a swift recollection of the stage-driver's account of his discovery.

"They say," continued Slinn, tremblingly, "that I never recovered my senses or consciousness for nearly three years; they *say* I lost my memory completely during my illness, and that by God's mercy, while I lay in that hospital, I knew no more than a babe; they say, because I could not speak or move, and only had my food as nature required it, that I was an imbecile, and that I never really came to my senses until after my son found me in the hospital. They *say* that — but I tell you to-night, Alvin Mulrady," he said, raising his voice to a hoarse outcry, "I tell you that it is a lie! I came to my senses a week after I lay on that hospital cot; I kept my senses and memory ever after during the three years that I was there, until Harry brought his cold, hypocritical face to my bedside and recognized me. Do you understand? I, the possessor of millions, lay there a pauper! Deserted by wife and children — a spectacle for the curious, a sport for the doctors — *and I knew it!* I heard them speculate on the cause of my helplessness. I heard them talk of excesses and indulgences — I, that never knew wine or woman! I heard a preacher speak of the finger of God, and point to me. May God curse him!"

"Go slow, old man; go slow," said Mulrady, gently.

"I heard them speak of me as a friendless man, an outcast, a criminal — a being whom no one would claim. They were right; no one claimed me. The friends of others visited them; relations came and took away their kindred; a few lucky ones got well; a few, equally lucky, died! I alone lived on, uncared for, deserted.

"The first year," he went on more rapidly, "I prayed for their coming. I looked for them every day. I never lost hope. I said to myself, 'She has not got my letter; but when the time passes she will be alarmed by my silence, and then she will come or send some one to seek me.' A young student got interested in my case, and, by studying my eyes, thought that I was not entirely imbecile and unconscious. With the aid of an alphabet, he got me to spell my name and town in Illinois, and promised by signs to write to my family. But in an evil moment I told him of my cursed fortune, and in that moment I saw that he thought me a fool and an idiot. He went away, and I saw him no more. Yet I still hoped. I dreamed of their joy at finding me, and the reward that my wealth would give them. Perhaps I was a little weak still, perhaps a little flighty, too, at times; but I was quite happy that year, even in my disappointment, for I had still hope!"

He paused, and again composed his face with his paralyzed hand; but his manner had become less excited, and his voice was stronger.

"A change must have come over me the second year, for I only dreaded their coming now and finding me so altered. A horrible idea that they might, like the student, believe me crazy if I spoke of my fortune made me pray to God that they might not reach me until after I had regained my health and strength — and found my fortune. When the third year found me still there — I no longer prayed for them — I cursed them! I swore to myself that they should never enjoy my wealth; but I wanted to live, and let them know I had it. I found myself getting stronger; but as I had no money, no friends, and nowhere to go, I concealed my real condition from the doctors, except to give them my name, and to try to get some little work to do to enable me to leave the hospital and seek my lost treasure. One day I found out by accident that it had been discovered! You understand — my treasure! — that had cost me years of labor and my reason; had left me a helpless, forgotten pauper. That gold I had never enjoyed had been found and taken possession of by another!"

He checked an exclamation from Mulrady with his hand. "They say they picked me up senseless from the floor, where I must have fallen when I heard the news — I don't remember — I recall nothing until I was confronted, nearly three weeks after, by my son, who had called at the hospital, as a reporter for a paper, and had accidentally discovered me through my name and appearance. He thought me crazy, or a fool. I did n't undeceive him. I did not tell him the story of the mine to excite his doubts and derision, or, worse (if I could bring proof to claim it), have it perhaps pass into his ungrateful hands. No; I said nothing. I let him bring me here. He could do no less, and common decency obliged him to do that."

"And what proof could you show of your claim?" asked Mulrady, gravely.

"If I had that letter — if I could find Masters," began Slinn, vaguely.

"Have you any idea where the letter is, or what has become of Masters?" continued Mulrady, with a matter-of-fact gravity, that seemed to increase Slinn's vagueness and excite his irritability.

"I don't know — I sometimes think" — He stopped, sat down again, and passed his hands across his forehead. "I have seen the letter somewhere since. Yes," he went on, with sudden vehemence, "I know it, I have seen it! I" — His brows knitted, his features began to work convulsively; he suddenly brought his paralyzed hand down, partly opened, upon the table. "I *will* remember where."

"Go slow, old man; go slow."

"You asked me once about my visions. Well, that is one of them. I remember a man somewhere showing me that letter. I have taken it from his hands and opened it, and knew it was mine by the specimens of gold that were in it. But where — or when — or what became of it, I cannot tell. It will come to me — it *must* come to me soon."

He turned his eyes upon Mulrady, who was regarding him with an expression of grave curiosity, and said bitterly, "You think me crazy. I know it. It needed only this."

"Where is this mine?" asked Mulrady, without heeding him.

The old man's eyes swiftly sought the ground.

"It is a secret, then?"

"No."

"You have spoken of it to any one?"

"No."

"Not to the man who possesses it?"

"No."

"Why?"

"Because I would n't take it from him."

"Why would n't you?"

"Because that man is yourself!"

In the instant of complete silence that followed they could hear that the monotonous patter of rain on the roof had ceased.

"Then all this was in *my* shaft, and the vein I thought I struck there was *your* lead, found three years ago in *your* tunnel. Is that your idea?"

"Yes."

"Then I don't *sabe* why you don't want to claim it."

"I have told you why I don't want it for my children. I go further, now, and I tell you, Alvin Mulrady, that I was willing that your children should squander it, as they were doing. It has only been a curse to me; it could only be a curse to them; but I thought you were happy in seeing it feed selfishness and vanity. You think me bitter and hard. Well, I should have left you in your fool's paradise, but that I saw to-night, when you came here, that your eyes had been opened like mine. You, the possessor of my wealth, my treasure, could not buy your children's loving care and company with your millions, any more than I could keep mine in my poverty. You were to-night lonely and forsaken, as I was. We were equal, for the first time in our lives. If that cursed gold had dropped down the shaft between us into the hell from which it sprang, we might have clasped hands like brothers across the chasm."

Mulrady, who in a friendly show of being at his ease had not yet resumed his coat, rose in his shirt-sleeves, and, standing before the hearth, straightened his square figure by drawing down his waistcoat on each side with two powerful thumbs. After a moment's contemplative survey of the floor between him and the speaker, he raised his eyes to Slinn. They were small and colorless; the forehead above them was low, and crowned with a shock of tawny reddish hair; even the rude strength of his lower features was enfeebled by a long, straggling, goat-like beard; but for the first time in his life the whole face was impressed and transformed with a strong and simple dignity.

"Ez far ez I kin see, Slinn," he said, gravely, "the pint between you and me ain't to be settled by our children, or wot we allow is doo and right from them to us. Afore we preach at them for playing in the slumgullion, and gettin' themselves splashed, perhaps we mout ez well remember that that thar slumgullion comes from our own sluice-boxes, where we wash our gold. So we'll just put *them* behind us, so," he continued, with a backward sweep of his powerful hand towards the chimney, "and goes on. The next thing that crops up ahead of us is your three years in the hospital, and wot you went through at that time. I ain't sayin' it wasn't rough on you, and that you didn't have it about as big as it's made; but ez you'll allow that you'd hev had that for three years, whether I'd found your mine or whether I had n't, I think we can put *that* behind us, too. There's nothin' now left to prospect but your story of your strike. Well, take your own proofs. Masters is not here; and if he was, accordin' to your own story, he knows nothin' of your strike that day, and could only prove you were a disappointed prospector in a tunnel; your letter — that the person you wrote to never got — *you* can't produce; and if you did, would be only your own story without proof! There is not a business man ez would look at your claim; there is n't a friend of yours that would n't believe you were crazy, and dreamed it all; there is n't a rival of yours ez would n't say ez you 'd invented it. Slinn, I 'm a business man — I am your friend — I am your rival — but I don't think you 're lyin' — I don't think you 're crazy — and I 'm not sure your claim ain't a good one!

"Ef you reckon from that that I 'm goin' to hand you over the mine to-morrow," he went on, after a pause, raising his hand with a deprecating gesture, "you 're mistaken. For your own sake, and the sake of my wife and children, you've got to prove it more clearly than you hev; but I promise you that from this night forward I will spare neither time nor money to help you to do it. I have more than doubled the amount that you would have had, had you taken the mine the day you came from the hospital. When you prove to me that your story is true — and we will find some way to prove it, if it *is* true — that amount will be yours at once, without the need of a word from law or lawyers. If you want my name to that in black and white, come to the office to-morrow, and you shall have it."

"And you think I'll take it now?" said the old man passionately. "Do you think that your charity will bring back my dead wife, the three years of my lost life, the love and respect of my children? Or do you think that your own wife and children, who deserted you in your wealth, will come back to you in your poverty? No! Let the mine stay, with its curse, where it is — I'll have none of it!"

"Go slow, old man; go slow," said Mulrady, quietly, putting on his coat. "You will take the mine if it is yours; if it is n't, I'll keep it. If it is yours, you will give your children a chance to show what they can do for you in your sudden prosperity, as I shall give mine a chance to show how they can stand reverse and disappointment. If my head is level — and I reckon it is — they'll both pan out all right."

He turned and opened the door. With a quick revulsion of feeling, Slinn suddenly seized Mulrady's hand between both of his own, and raised it to his lips. Mulrady smiled, disengaged his hand gently, and saying soothingly, "Go slow, old man; go slow," closed the door behind him, and passed out into the clear Christmas dawn.

For the stars, with the exception of one that seemed to sparkle brightly over the shaft of his former fortunes, were slowly paling. A burden seemed to have fallen from his square shoulders as he stepped out sturdily into the morning air. He had already forgotten the lonely man behind him, for he was thinking only of his wife and daughter.

And at the same moment they were thinking of him; and in their elaborate villa overlooking the blue Mediterranean at Cannes were discussing, in the event of Mamie's marriage with Prince Rosso e Negro, the possibility of Mr. Mulrady's paying two hundred and fifty thousand dollars, the gambling debts of that unfortunate but deeply conscientious nobleman.

CHAPTER VI.

When Alvin Mulrady reëntered his own house, he no longer noticed its loneliness. Whether the events of the last few hours had driven it from his mind, or whether his late reflections had repeopled it with his family under pleasanter auspices, it would be difficult to determine. Destitute as he was of imagination, and matter-of-fact in his judgments, he realized his new situation as calmly as he would have considered any business proposition. While he was decided to act upon his moral convictions purely, he was prepared to submit the facts of Slinn's claim to the usual patient and laborious investigation of his practical mind. It was the least he could do to justify the ready and almost superstitious assent he had given to Slinn's story.

When he had made a few memoranda at his desk by the growing light, he again took the key of the attic, and ascended to the loft that held the tangible memories of his past life. If he was still under the influence of his reflections, it was with very different sensations that he now regarded them. Was it possible that these ashes might be warmed again, and these scattered embers rekindled? His practical sense said No! whatever his wish might have been. A sudden chill came over him; he began to realize the terrible change that was probable, more by the impossibility of his accepting the old order of things than by his voluntarily abandoning the new. His wife and children would never submit. They would go away from this place, far away, where no reminiscence of either former wealth or former poverty could obtrude itself upon them. Mamie — his Mamie — should never go back to the cabi ., since desecrated by Slinn's daughters, and take their places. No! Why should she? — because of the half-sick, half-crazy dreams of an old vindictive man?

He stopped suddenly. In moodily turning over a heap of mining clothing, blankets, and india-rubber boots, he had come upon an old pickaxe — the one he had found in the shaft; the one he had carefully preserved for a year, and then forgotten! Why had he not remembered it before? He was frightened, not only at this sudden resurrection of the proof he was seeking, but at his own fateful forgetfulness. Why had he never thought of this when Slinn was speaking? A sense of shame, as if he had voluntarily withheld it from the wronged man, swept over him. He was turning away, when he was again startled.

This time it was by a voice from below — a voice calling him — Slinn's voice. How had the crippled man got here so soon, and what did he want? He hurriedly laid aside the pick, which, in his first impulse, he had taken to the door of the loft with him, and descended the stairs. The old man was standing at the door of his office awaiting him.

As Mulrady approached, he trembled violently, and clung to the doorpost for support.

"I had to come over, Mulrady," he said, in a choked voice; "I could stand it there no longer. I've come to beg you to forget all that I have said; to drive all thought of what passed between us last night out of your head and mine forever! I've come to ask you to swear with me that neither of us will ever speak of this again forever. It is not worth the happiness I have had in your friendship for the last half-year; it is not worth the agony I have suffered in its loss in the last half-hour."

Mulrady grasped his outstretched hand. "P'raps," he said, gravely, "there may n't be any use for another word, if you can answer one now. Come with me. No matter," he added, as Slinn moved with difficulty; "I will help you."

He half supported, half lifted the paralyzed man up the three flights of stairs, and opened the door of the loft. The pick was leaning against the wall, where he had left it. "Look around, and see if you recognize anything."

The old man's eyes fell upon the implement in a half-frightened way, and then lifted themselves interrogatively to Mulrady's face.

"Do you know that pick?"

Slinn raised it in his trembling hands. "I think I do; and yet" —

"Slinn! is it yours?"

"No," he said, hurriedly.

"Then what makes you think you know it?"

"It has a short handle like one I've seen."

"And it isn't yours?"

"No. The handle of mine was broken and spliced. I was too poor to buy a new one."

"Then you say that this pick which I found in my shaft is not yours?"

"Yes."

"Slinn!"

The old man passed his hand across his forehead, looked at Mulrady, and dropped his eyes. "It is not mine," he said simply.

"That will do," said Mulrady, gravely.

"And you will not speak of this again?" said the old man, timidly.

"I promise you — not until I have some more evidence."

He kept his word, but not before he had extorted from Slinn as full a description of Masters as his imperfect memory and still more imperfect knowledge of his former neighbor could furnish. He placed this, with a large sum of money and the promise of a still larger reward, in the hands of a trustworthy agent. When this was done he resumed his old relations with Slinn, with the exception that the domestic letters of Mrs. Mulrady and Mamie were no longer a subject of comment, and their bills no longer passed through his private secretary's hands.

Three months passed; the rainy season had ceased, the hillsides around Mulrady's shaft were bridal-like with flowers; indeed, there were rumors of an approaching fashionable marriage in the air, and vague hints in the "Record" that the presence of a distinguished capitalist might soon be required abroad. The face of that distinguished man did not, however, reflect the gayety of nature nor the anticipation of happiness; on the contrary, for the past few weeks, he had appeared disturbed and anxious, and that rude tranquillity which had characterized him was wanting. People shook their heads; a few suggested speculations; all agreed on extravagance.

One morning, after office hours, Slinn, who had been watching the careworn face of his employer, suddenly rose and limped to his side.

"We promised each other," he said, in a voice trembling with emotion, "never to allude to our talk of Christmas Eve again unless we had other proofs of what I told you then. We have none; I don't believe we'll ever have any more. I don't care if we ever do, and I break that promise now because I cannot bear to see you unhappy and know that this is the cause."

Mulrady made a motion of deprecation, but the old man continued:—

"You are unhappy, Alvin Mulrady. You are unhappy because you want to give your daughter a dowry of two hundred and fifty thousand dollars, and you will not use the fortune that you think may be mine."

"Who's been talking about a dowry?" asked Mulrady, with an angry flush.

"Don Cæsar Alvarado told my daughter."

"Then that is why he has thrown off on me since he returned," said Mulrady, with sudden small malevolence, "just that he might unload his gossip because Mamie would n't have him. The old woman was right in warnin' me agin him."

The outburst was so unlike him, and so dwarfed his large though common nature with its littleness, that it was easy to detect its feminine origin, although it filled Slinn with vague alarm.

"Never mind him," said the old man, hastily; "what I wanted to say now is that I abandon everything to you and yours. There are no proofs; there never will be any more than what we know, than what we have tested and found wanting. I swear to you that, except to show you that I have not lied and am not crazy, I would destroy them on their way to your hands. Keep the money, and spend it as you will. Make your daughter happy, and, through her, yourself. You have made me happy through your liberality; don't make me suffer through your privation."

" I tell you what, old man," said Mulrady, rising to his feet, with an awkward mingling of frankness and shame in his manner and accent, " I should like to pay that money for Mamie, and let her be a princess, if it would make her happy. I should like to shut the lantern jaws of that Don Cæsar, who 'd be too glad if anything happened to break off Mamie's match. But I should n't touch that capital — unless you 'd lend it to me. If you 'll take a note from me, payable if the property ever becomes yours, I 'd thank you. A mortgage on the old house and garden, and the lands I bought of Don Cæsar, outside the mine, will screen you."

" If that pleases you," said the old man, with a smile, " have your way; and if I tear up the note, it does not concern you."

It did please the distinguished capitalist of Rough-and-Ready; for the next few days his face wore a brightened expression, and he seemed to have recovered his old tranquillity. There was, in fact, a slight touch of consequence in his manner, the first ostentation he had ever indulged in, when he was informed one morning at his private office that Don Cæsar Alvarado was in the counting-house, desiring a few moments' conference. "Tell him to come in," said Mulrady, shortly. The door opened upon Don Cæsar — erect, sallow, and grave. Mulrady had not seen him since his return from Europe, and even his inexperienced eyes were struck with the undeniable ease and grace with which the young Spanish-American had assimilated the style and fashion of an older civilization. It seemed rather as if he had returned to a familiar condition than adopted a new one.

"Take a cheer," said Mulrady.

The young man looked at Slinn with quietly persistent significance.

"You can talk all the same," said Mulrady, accepting the significance. "He's my private secretary."

"It seems that for that reason we might choose another moment for our conversation," returned Don Cæsar, haughtily. "Do I understand you cannot see me now?"

Mulrady hesitated. He had always revered and recognized a certain social superiority in Don Ramon Alvarado; somehow his son — a young man of half his age, and once a possible son-in-law — appeared to claim that recognition also. He rose, without a word, and preceded Don Cæsar up-stairs into his drawing-room. The alien portrait on the wall seemed to evidently take sides with Don Cæsar, as against the common intruder, Mulrady.

"I hoped the Señora Mulrady might have saved me this interview," said the young man, stiffly; "or at least have given you some intimation of the reason why I seek it. As you just now proposed my talking to you in the presence of the unfortunate Señor Esslinn himself, it appears she has not."

"I don't know what you're driving at, or

what Mrs. Mulrady's got to do with Slinn or you," said Mulrady, in angry uneasiness.

"Do I understand," said Don Cæsar, sternly, "that Señora Mulrady has not told you that I entrusted to her an important letter, belonging to Señor Esslinn, which I had the honor to discover in the wood six months ago, and which she said she would refer to you?"

"Letter?" echoed Mulrady, slowly; "my wife had a letter of Slinn's?"

Don Cæsar regarded the millionaire attentively. "It is as I feared," he said, gravely. "You do not know, or you would not have remained silent." He then briefly recounted the story of his finding Slinn's letter, his exhibition of it to the invalid, its disastrous effect upon him, and his innocent discovery of the contents. "I believed myself at that time on the eve of being allied with your family, Señor Mulrady," he said, haughtily; "and when I found myself in possession of a secret which affected its integrity and good name, I did not choose to leave it in the helpless hands of its imbecile owner, or his sillier children, but proposed to trust it to the care of the Señora, that she and you might deal with it as became your honor and mine. I followed her to Paris, and gave her the letter there. She affected to laugh at any pretension of the writer, or any claim he might have on your bounty; but she kept the letter, and, I fear, destroyed it. You will understand, Señor Mulrady, that when I found that my attentions were no longer agreeable to your daughter, I had no longer the right to speak to you on the subject, nor could I, without misapprehension, force her to return it. I should have still kept the secret to myself, if I had not since my return here made the nearer acquaintance of Señor Esslinn's daughters. I cannot present myself at his house, as a suitor for the hand of the Señorita Vashti, until I have asked his absolution for my complicity in the wrong that has been done to him. I cannot, as a *caballero*, do that without your permission. It is for that purpose I am here."

It needed only this last blow to complete

the humiliation that whitened Mulrady's face. But his eye was none the less clear and his voice none the less steady as he turned to Don Cæsar.

"You know perfectly the contents of that letter?"

"I have kept a copy of it."

"Come with me."

He preceded his visitor down the staircase and back into his private office. Slinn looked up at his employer's face in unrestrained anxiety. Mulrady sat down at his desk, wrote a few hurried lines, and rang a bell. A manager appeared from the counting-room.

"Send that to the bank."

He wiped his pen as methodically as if he had not at that moment countermanded the order to pay his daughter's dowry, and turned quietly to Slinn.

"Don Cæsar Alvarado has found the letter you wrote your wife on the day you made your strike in the tunnel that is now my shaft. He gave the letter to Mrs. Mulrady; but he has kept a copy."

Unheeding the frightened gesture of entreaty from Slinn, equally with the unfeigned astonishment of Don Cæsar, who was entirely unprepared for this revelation of Mulrady's and Slinn's confidences, he continued, " He has brought the copy with him. I reckon it would be only square for you to compare it with what you remember of the original."

In obedience to a gesture from Mulrady, Don Cæsar mechanically took from his pocket a folded paper, and handed it to the paralytic. But Slinn's trembling fingers could scarcely unfold the paper; and as his eyes fell upon its contents, his convulsive lips could not articulate a word.

" P'raps I 'd better read it for you," said Mulrady, gently. " You kin follow me and stop me when I go wrong."

He took the paper, and, in a dead silence, read as follows: —

" DEAR WIFE, — I 've just struck gold in my tunnel, and you must get ready to come here with the children, at once. It was after six months' hard work; and I 'm so weak I

... It's a fortune for us all. We should be rich even if it were only a branch vein dipping west towards the next tunnel, instead of dipping east, according to my theory" —

"Stop!" said Slinn, in a voice that shook the room.

Mulrady looked up.

"It's wrong, ain't it?" he asked, anxiously; "it should be *east* towards the next tunnel."

"No! *It's right! I* am wrong! We're all wrong!"

Slinn had risen to his feet, erect and inspired. "Don't you see," he almost screamed, with passionate vehemence, "it's *Masters' abandoned tunnel* your shaft has struck? Not mine! It was Masters' pick you found! I know it now!"

"And your own tunnel?" said Mulrady, springing to his feet in his excitement. "And *your* strike?"

"Is still there!"

The next instant, and before another question could be asked, Slinn had darted from the room. In the exaltation of that supreme discovery he regained the full control of mind and body. Mulrady and Don Cæsar, no less excited, followed him precipitately, and with difficulty kept up with his feverish speed. Their way lay along the base of the hill below Mulrady's shaft, and on a line with Masters' abandoned tunnel. Only once he stopped to snatch a pick from the hand of an astonished Chinaman at work in a ditch, as he still kept on his way, a quarter of a mile beyond the shaft. Here he stopped before a jagged hole in the hillside. Bared to the sky and air, the very openness of its abandonment, its unpropitious position, and distance from the strike in Mulrady's shaft had no doubt preserved its integrity from wayfarer or prospector.

"You can't go in there alone, and without a light," said Mulrady, laying his hand on the arm of the excited man. "Let me get more help and proper tools."

"I know every step in the dark as in the daylight," returned Slinn, struggling. "Let me go, while I have yet strength and reason! Stand aside!"

He broke from them, and the next moment was swallowed up in the yawning blackness. They waited with bated breath until, after a seeming eternity of night and silence, they heard his returning footsteps, and ran forward to meet him. As he was carrying something clasped to his breast, they supported him to the opening. But at the same moment the object of his search, and his burden, a misshapen wedge of gold and quartz, dropped with him, and both fell together with equal immobility to the ground. He had still strength to turn his fading eyes to the other millionaire of Rough-and-Ready, who leaned over him.

"You — see," he gasped, brokenly, "I was not — crazy!"

No. He was dead!

DEVIL'S FORD.

CHAPTER I.

It was a season of unequalled prosperity in Devil's Ford. The half a dozen cabins scattered along the banks of the North Fork, as if by some overflow of that capricious river, had become augmented during a week of fierce excitement by twenty or thirty others, that were huddled together on the narrow gorge of Devil's Spur, or cast up on its steep sides. So sudden and violent had been the change of fortune, that the dwellers in the older cabins had not had time to change with it, but still kept their old habits, customs, and even their old clothes. The flour pan in which their daily bread was mixed stood on the rude table side by side with the " prospecting pans," half full of gold washed up from their morning's work; the front windows of the newer tenements looked upon the one single thoroughfare, but the back door opened upon the uncleared wilderness, still haunted by the misshapen bulk of bear or the nightly gliding of catamount.

Neither had success as yet affected their boyish simplicity and the frankness of old frontier habits; they played with their new-found riches with the naive delight of children, and rehearsed their glowing future with the importance and triviality of school-boys.

"I've bin kalklatin'," said Dick Mattingly, leaning on his long-handled shovel with lazy gravity, "that when I go to Rome this winter, I'll get one o' them marble sharps to chisel me a statoo o' some kind to set up on the spot where we made our big strike. Suthin' to remember it by, you know."

"What kind o' statoo — Washington or Webster?" asked one of the Kearney brothers, without looking up from his work.

"No — I reckon one o' them fancy groups — one o' them Latin goddesses that Fairfax is always gassin' about, sorter leadin', directin', and bossin' us where to dig."

"You 'd make a healthy-lookin' figger in a group," responded Kearney, critically regarding an enormous patch in Mattingly's trousers. "Why don't you have a fountain instead?"

"Where 'll you get the water?" demanded the first speaker, in return. "You know there ain't enough in the North Fork to do a week's washing for the camp — to say nothin' of its color."

"Leave that to me," said Kearney, with self-possession. "When I 've built that there reservoir on Devil's Spur, and bring the water over the ridge from Union Ditch, there 'll be enough to spare for that."

"Better mix it up, I reckon — have suthin' half statoo, half fountain," interposed the elder Mattingly, better known as "Maryland Joe," "and set it up afore the Town Hall and Free Library I 'm kalklatin' to give. Do *that*, and you can count on me."

After some further discussion, it was gravely settled that Kearney should furnish water brought from the Union Ditch, twenty miles away, at a cost of two hundred thousand dollars, to feed a memorial fountain erected by Mattingly, worth a hundred thousand dollars, as a crowning finish to public buildings contributed by Maryland Joe, to the extent of half a million more. The disposition of these vast sums by gentlemen wearing patched breeches awakened no sense of the ludicrous, nor did any doubt, reservation, or contingency enter into the plans of the charming enthusiasts themselves. The foundation of their airy castles lay already before them in the strip of rich alluvium on the river bank, where the North Fork, sharply curving round the base of Devil's Spur, had for centuries swept the detritus of gulch and canon. They had barely crossed the threshold of this treasure-house, to find themselves rich men; what possibilities of affluence might be theirs when they had fully exploited their possessions? So confident were they of that ultimate prospect, that the wealth already thus obtained was religiously expended in engines and machinery for the boring of wells and the conveyance of that precious water which the exhausted river had long since ceased to yield. It seemed as if the gold they had taken out was by some ironical compensation gradually making its way back to the soil again through ditch and flume and reservoir.

Such was the position of affairs at Devil's Ford on the 13th of August, 1860. It was noon of a hot day. Whatever movement there was in the stifling air was seen rather than felt in a tremulous, quivering, upward-moving dust along the flank of the mountain, through which the spires of the pines were faintly visible. There was no water in the bared and burning bars of the river to reflect the vertical sun, but under its direct rays one or two tinned roofs and corrugated zinc cabins struck fire, a few canvas tents became dazzling to the eye, and the white wooded corral of the stage office and hotel insupportable. For two hours no one ventured in the glare of the open, or even to cross the narrow, unshadowed street, whose dull red dust seemed to glow between the lines of straggling houses. The heated shells of these green unseasoned tenements gave out a pungent odor of scorching wood and resin. The usual hurried, feverish toil in the claim was suspended; the pick and shovel were left sticking in the richest " pay gravel; " the toiling millionaires themselves, ragged, dirty, and perspiring, lay panting under the nearest shade, where their pipes went out listlessly, and conversation sank to monosyllables.

" There's Fairfax," said Dick Mattingly, at last, with a lazy effort. His face was turned to the hillside, where a man had just emerged from the woods, and was halting irresolutely before the glaring expanse of upheaved gravel and glistening boulders that stretched between him and the shaded group. " He's going to make a break for it," he added, as the stranger, throwing his linen coat over his head, suddenly started into an Indian trot through the pelting sunbeams toward them. This strange act was perfectly understood by the group, who knew that in that intensely dry heat the danger of exposure was lessened by active exercise and the profuse perspiration that followed it. In another moment the stranger had reached their side, dripping as if rained upon, mopping his damp curls and handsome bearded face with his linen coat, as he threw himself pantingly on the ground.

"I struck out over here first, boys, to give you a little warning," he said, as soon as he had gained breath. "That engineer will be down here to take charge as soon as the six o'clock stage comes in. He's an oldish chap, has got a family of two daughters, and — I — am — d——d if he is not bringing them down here with him."

"Oh, go long!" exclaimed the five men in one voice, raising themselves on their hands and elbows, and glaring at the speaker.

"Fact, boys! Soon as I found it out I just waltzed into that Jew shop at the Crossing and bought up all the clothes that would be likely to suit you fellows, before anybody else got a show. I reckon I cleared out the shop. The duds are a little mixed in style, but I reckon they're clean and whole, and a man might face a lady in 'em. I left them round at the old Buckeye Spring, where they're handy without attracting attention. You boys can go there for a general wash-up, rig yourselves up without saying anything, and then meander back careless and easy in your store clothes, just as the stage is coming in, *sabe?*"

"Why did n't you let us know earlier?" asked Mattingly aggrievedly; "you've been back here at least an hour."

"I've been getting some place ready for *them*," returned the new-comer. "We might have managed to put the man somewhere, if he'd been alone, but these women want family accommodation. There was nothing left for me to do but to buy up Thompson's saloon."

"No?" interrupted his audience, half in incredulity, half in protestation.

"Fact! You boys will have to take your drinks under canvas again, I reckon! But I made Thompson let those gold-framed mirrors that used to stand behind the bar go into the bargain, and they sort of furnish the room. You know the saloon is one of them patent houses you can take to pieces, and I've been reckoning you boys will have to pitch in and help me to take the whole shanty over to the laurel bushes, and put it up agin Kearney's cabin."

"What's all that?" said the younger Kearney, with an odd mingling of astonishment and bashful gratification.

"Yes, I reckon yours is the cleanest house, because it's the newest, so you'll just step out and let us knock in one o' the gables, and clap it on to the saloon, and make *one* house of it, don't you see? There'll be two rooms, one for the girls and the other for the old man."

The astonishment and bewilderment of the party had gradually given way to a boyish and impatient interest.

"Hadn't we better do the job at once?" suggested Dick Mattingly.

"Or throw ourselves into those new clothes, so as to be ready," added the younger Kearney, looking down at his ragged trousers. "I say, Fairfax, what are the girls like, eh?"

All the others had been dying to ask the

question, yet one and all laughed at the conscious manner and blushing cheek of the questioner.

"You'll find out quick enough," returned Fairfax, whose curt carelessness did not, however, prevent a slight increase of color on his own cheek. "We'd better get that job off our hands before doing anything else. So, if you're ready, boys, we'll just waltz down to Thompson's and pack up the shanty. He's out of it by this time, I reckon. You might as well be perspiring to some purpose over there as gaspin' under this tree. We won't go back to work this afternoon, but knock off now, and call it half a day. Come! Hump yourselves, gentlemen. Are you ready? One, two, three, and away!"

In another instant the tree was deserted; the figures of the five millionaires of Devil's Ford, crossing the fierce glare of the open space, with boyish alacrity, glistened in the sunlight, and then disappeared in the nearest fringe of thickets.

CHAPTER II.

Six hours later, when the shadow of Devil's Spur had crossed the river, and spread a slight coolness over the flat beyond, the Pioneer coach, leaving the summit, began also to bathe its heated bulk in the long shadows of the descent. Conspicuous among the dusty passengers, the two pretty and youthful faces of the daughters of Philip Carr, mining superintendent and engineer, looked from the windows with no little anxiety towards their future home in the straggling settlement below, that occasionally came in view at the turns of the long zigzagging road. A slight look of comical disappointment passed between them as they gazed upon the sterile flat, dotted with unsightly excrescences that stood equally for cabins or mounds of stone and gravel. It was so feeble and inconsistent a culmination to the beautiful scenery they had passed through, so hopeless and imbecile a conclusion to the preparation of that long picturesque journey, with its glimpses of sylvan and pastoral glades and cañons, that, as the coach swept down the last incline, and the remorseless monotony of the dead level spread out before them, furrowed by ditches and indented by pits, under cover of shielding their cheeks from the impalpable dust that rose beneath the plunging wheels, they buried their faces in their handkerchiefs, to hide a few half-hysterical tears. Happily, their father, completely absorbed in a practical, scientific, and approving contemplation of the topography and material resources of the scene of his future labors, had no time to notice their defection. It was not until the stage drew up before a rambling tenement bearing the inscription, " Hotel and Stage Office," that he became fully aware of it.

"We can't stop *here*, papa," said Christie Carr decidedly, with a shake of her pretty head. "You can't expect that."

Mr. Carr looked up at the building; it was half grocery, half saloon. Whatever other accommodation it contained must have been hidden in the rear, as the flat roof above was almost level with the raftered ceiling of the shop.

"Certainly," he replied hurriedly; "we'll see to that in a moment. I dare say it's all right. I told Fairfax we were coming. Somebody ought to be here."

"But they're not," said Jessie Carr indignantly; "and the few that were here scampered off like rabbits to their burrows as soon as they saw us get down."

It was true. The little group of loungers before the building had suddenly disappeared. There was the flash of a red shirt vanishing in an adjacent doorway; the fading apparition of a pair of high boots and blue overalls in another; the abrupt withdrawal of a curly blonde head from a sashless window over the way. Even the saloon was deserted, although a back door in the dim recess seemed to creak mysteriously. The stage-coach, with the other passengers, had already rattled away.

"I certainly think Fairfax understood that I"— began Mr. Carr.

He was interrupted by the pressure of Christie's fingers on his arm and a subdued exclamation from Jessie, who was staring down the street.

"What are they?" she whispered in her sister's ear. "Nigger minstrels, a circus, or what?"

The five millionaires of Devil's Ford had just turned the corner of the straggling street, and were approaching in single file. One glance was sufficient to show that they had already availed themselves of the new clothing bought by Fairfax, had washed, and one or two had shaved. But the result was startling.

Through some fortunate coincidence in size, Dick Mattingly was the only one who had achieved an entire suit. But it was of funereal black cloth, and although relieved at one extremity by a pair of high riding boots, in which his too short trousers were tucked, and at the other by a tall white hat, and cravat of aggressive yellow, the effect was depressing. In agreeable contrast, his brother, Maryland Joe, was attired in a thin fawn-colored summer overcoat, lightly worn open, so as to show the unstarched bosom of a white embroidered shirt, and a pair of nankeen trousers and pumps. The Kearney brothers had divided a suit between them, the elder wearing a tightly-fitting, single-breasted blue frock-coat and a pair of pink striped cotton trousers, while the younger candidly displayed the trousers of his brother's suit, as a harmonious change to a shining black alpaca coat and crimson neckerchief. Fairfax, who brought up the rear, had, with characteristic unselfishness, contented himself with a French workman's blue blouse and a pair of white duck trousers. Had they shown the least consciousness of their finery, or of its absurdity, they would have seemed despicable. But only one expression beamed on the five sunburnt and shining faces — a look of unaffected boyish gratification and unrestricted welcome.

They halted before Mr. Carr and his daughters, simultaneously removed their various and remarkable head coverings, and waited until Fairfax advanced and severally presented them. Jessie Carr's half-frightened smile took refuge in the trembling shadows of her dark lashes; Christie Carr stiffened slightly, and looked straight before her.

"We reckoned — that is — we intended to meet you and the young ladies at the grade," said Fairfax, reddening a little as he endeavored to conceal his too ready slang, "and save you from trapesing — from dragging yourselves up grade again to your house."

"Then there *is* a house?" said Jessie, with an alarmingly frank laugh of relief, that was, however, as frankly reflected in the boyishly appreciative eyes of the young men.

"Such as it is," responded Fairfax, with a shade of anxiety, as he glanced at the fresh and pretty costumes of the young women, and dubiously regarded the two Saratoga trunks resting hopelessly on the veranda. "I'm afraid it is n't much, for what you 're accustomed to. But," he added more cheerfully, " it will do for a day or two, and perhaps you'll give us the pleasure of showing you the way there now."

The procession was quickly formed. Mr. Carr, alive only to the actual business that had brought him there, at once took possession of Fairfax, and began to disclose his plans for the working of the mine, occasionally halting to look at the work already done in the ditches, and to examine the field of his future operations. Fairfax, not displeased at being thus relieved of a lighter attendance on Mr. Carr's daughters, nevertheless from time to time cast a paternal glance backwards upon their escorts, who had each seized a handle of the two trunks, and were carrying them in couples at the young ladies' side. The occupation did not offer much freedom for easy gallantry, but no sign of discomfiture or uneasiness was visible in the grateful faces of the young men. The necessity of changing hands at times with their burdens brought a corresponding change of cavalier at the lady's side, although it was observed that the younger

Kearney, for the sake of continuing a conversation with Miss Jessie, kept his grasp of the handle nearest the young lady until his hand was nearly cut through, and his arm worn out by exhaustion.

"The only thing on wheels in the camp is a mule wagon, and the mules are packin' gravel from the river this afternoon," explained Dick Mattingly apologetically to Christie, "or we'd have toted — I mean carried — you and your baggage up to the shant — the — your house. Give us two weeks more, Miss Carr — only two weeks to wash up our work and realize — and we'll give you a pair of 2.40 steppers and a skeleton buggy to meet you at the top of the hill and drive you over to the cabin. Perhaps you'd prefer a regular carriage; some ladies do. And a nigger driver. But what's the use of planning anything? Afore that time comes we'll have run you up a house on the hill, and you shall pick out the spot. It wouldn't take long — unless you preferred brick. I suppose we could get brick over from La Grange, if you cared for it, but it would take longer. If you could put up for a time with something of stained glass and a mahogany veranda " —

In spite of her cold indignation, and the fact that she could understand only a part of Mattingly's speech, Christie comprehended enough to make her lift her clear eyes to the speaker, as she replied freezingly that she feared she would not trouble them long with her company.

"Oh, you 'll get over that," responded Mattingly, with an exasperating confidence that drove her nearly frantic, from the manifest kindliness of intent that made it impossible for her to resent it. "I felt that way myself at first. Things will look strange and unsociable for a while, until you get the hang of them. You 'll naturally stamp round and cuss a little" — he stopped in conscious consternation.

With ready tact, and before Christie could reply, Maryland Joe had put down the trunk and changed hands with his brother.

"You must n't mind Dick, or he 'll go off and kill himself with shame," he whispered laughingly in her ear. "He means all right, but he's picked up so much slang here he's about forgotten how to talk English, and it's nigh on to four years since he's met a young lady."

Christie did not reply. Yet the laughter of her sister in advance with the Kearney brothers seemed to make the reserve with which she tried to crush further familiarity only ridiculous.

"Do you know many operas, Miss Carr?"

She looked at the boyish, interested, sunburnt face so near to her own, and hesitated. After all, why should she add to her other real disappointments by taking this absurd creature seriously?

"In what way?" she returned, with a half smile.

"To play. On the piano, of course. There is n't one nearer here than Sacramento; but I reckon we could get a small one by Thursday. You could n't do anything on a banjo?" he added doubtfully; "Kearney's got one."

"I imagine it would be very difficult to

carry a piano over those mountains," said Christie laughingly, to avoid the collateral of the banjo.

"We got a billiard-table over from Stockton," half bashfully interrupted Dick Mattingly, struggling from his end of the trunk to recover his composure, "and it had to be brought over in sections on the back of a mule, so I don't see why" — He stopped short again in confusion, at a sign from his brother, and then added, " I mean, of course, that a piano is a heap more delicate, and valuable, and all that sort of thing, but it's worth trying for."

"Fairfax was always saying he'd get one for himself, so I reckon it's possible," said Joe.

"Does he play?" asked Christie.

"You bet," said Joe, quite forgetting himself in his enthusiasm. "He can snatch Mozart and Beethoven bald-headed."

In the embarrassing silence that followed this speech the fringe of pine wood nearest the flat was reached. Here there was a rude "clearing," and beneath an enormous pine stood the two recently joined tenements.

There was no attempt to conceal the point of junction between Kearney's cabin and the newly-transported saloon from the flat — no architectural illusion of the palpable collusion of the two buildings, which seemed to be telescoped into each other. The front room or living room occupied the whole of Kearney's cabin. It contained, in addition to the necessary articles for housekeeping, a "bunk" or berth for Mr. Carr, so as to leave the second building entirely to the occupation of his daughters as bedroom and boudoir.

There was a half-humorous, half-apologetic exhibition of the rude utensils of the living room, and then the young men turned away as the two girls entered the open door of the second room. Neither Christie nor Jessie could for a moment understand the delicacy which kept these young men from accompanying them into the room they had but a few moments before decorated and arranged with their own hands, and it was not until they turned to thank their strange entertainers that they found that they were gone.

The arrangement of the second room was rude and *bizarre*, but not without a singular originality and even tastefulness of conception. What had been the counter or " bar " of the saloon, gorgeous in white and gold, now sawn in two and divided, was set up on opposite sides of the room as separate dressing-tables, decorated with huge bunches of azaleas, that hid the rough earthenware bowls, and gave each table the appearance of a vestal altar.

The huge gilt plate-glass mirror which had hung behind the bar still occupied one side of the room, but its length was artfully divided by an enormous rosette of red, white, and blue muslin — one of the surviving Fourth of July decorations of Thompson's saloon. On either side of the door two pathetic-looking, convent-like cots, covered with spotless sheeting, and heaped up in the middle, like a snow-covered grave, had attracted their attention. They were still staring at them when Mr. Carr anticipated their curiosity.

" I ought to tell you that the young men

confided to me the fact that there was neither bed nor mattress to be had on the Ford. They have filled some flour-sacks with clean dry moss from the woods, and put half a dozen blankets on the top, and they hope you can get along until the messenger who starts to-night for La Grange can bring some bedding over."

Jessie flew with mischievous delight to satisfy herself of the truth of this marvel. "It's so, Christie," she said laughingly — "three flour-sacks apiece; but I'm jealous: yours are all marked '*superfine*,' and mine '*middlings*.'"

Mr. Carr had remained uneasily watching Christie's shadowed face.

"What matters?" she said drily. "The accommodation is all in keeping."

"It will be better in a day or two," he continued, casting a longing look towards the door — the first refuge of masculine weakness in an impending domestic emergency. "I'll go and see what can be done," he said feebly, with a sidelong impulse towards the opening and freedom. "I've got to see Fairfax again to-night any way."

"One moment, father," said Christie, wearily. "Did you know anything of this place and these — these people — before you came?"

"Certainly — of course I did," he returned, with the sudden testiness of disturbed abstraction. "What are you thinking of? I knew the geological strata and the — the report of Fairfax and his partners before I consented to take charge of the works. And I can tell you that there is a fortune here. I intend to make my own terms, and share in it."

"And not take a salary or some sum of money down?" said Christie, slowly removing her bonnet in the same resigned way.

"I am not a hired man, or a workman, Christie," said her father sharply. "You ought not to oblige me to remind you of that."

"But the hired men — the superintendent and his workmen — were the only ones who ever got anything out of your last experiment with Colonel Waters at La Grange, and — and we at least lived among civilized people there."

"These young men are not common people, Christie; even if they have forgotten the restraints of speech and manners, they 're gentlemen."

"Who are willing to live like — like negroes."

"You can make them what you please."

Christie raised her eyes. There was a certain cynical ring in her father's voice that was unlike his usual hesitating abstraction. It both puzzled and pained her.

"I mean," he said hastily, "that you have the same opportunity to direct the lives of these young men into more regular, disciplined channels that I have to regulate and correct their foolish waste of industry and material here. It would at least beguile the time for you."

Fortunately for Mr. Carr's escape and Christie's uneasiness, Jessie, who had been examining the details of the living-room, broke in upon this conversation.

"I'm sure it will be as good as a perpetual picnic. George Kearney says we can have a cooking-stove under the tree outside at the back, and as there will be no rain for three months we can do the cooking there, and that will give us more room for — for the piano when it comes; and there's an old squaw to do the cleaning and washing-up any day — and — and — it will be real fun."

She stopped breathlessly, with glowing cheeks and sparkling eyes — a charming picture of youth and trustfulness. Mr. Carr had seized the opportunity to escape.

"Really, now, Christie," said Jessie confidentially, when they were alone, and Christie had begun to unpack her trunk, and to mechanically put her things away, "they're not so bad."

"Who?" asked Christie.

"Why, the Kearneys, and Mattinglys, and Fairfax, and the lot, provided you don't look at their clothes. And think of it! they told me — for they tell one *everything* in the most alarming way — that those clothes were bought to please *us*. A scramble of things bought at La Grange, without reference to size or style. And to hear these creatures talk, why, you'd think they were Astors or

Rothschilds. Think of that little one with the curls — I don't believe he's over seventeen, for all his baby moustache — says he's going to build an assembly hall for us to give a dance in next month; and apologizes the next breath to tell us that there isn't any milk to be had nearer than La Grange, and we must do without it, and use syrup in our tea to-morrow."

"And where is all this wealth?" said Christie, forcing herself to smile at her sister's animation.

"Under our very feet, my child, and all along the river. Why, what we thought was pure and simple mud is what they call 'gold-bearing cement.'"

"I suppose that is why they don't brush their boots and trousers, it's so precious," returned Christie drily. "And have they ever translated this precious dirt into actual coin?"

"Bless you, yes. Why, that dirty little gutter, you know, that ran along the side of the road and followed us down the hill all the way here, that cost them — let me see —

yes, nearly sixty thousand dollars. And fancy! papa's just condemned it — says it won't do; and they've got to build another."

An impatient sigh from Christie drew Jessie's attention to her troubled eyebrows.

"Don't worry about our disappointment, dear. It isn't so very great. I dare say we'll be able to get along here in some way, until papa is rich again. You know they intend to make him share with them."

"It strikes me that he is sharing with them already," said Christie, glancing bitterly round the cabin; "sharing everything — ourselves, our lives, our tastes."

"Ye-e-s!" said Jessie, with vaguely hesitating assent. "Yes, even these:" she showed two dice in the palm of her little hand. "I found 'em in the drawer of our dressing-table."

"Throw them away," said Christie impatiently.

But Jessie's small fingers closed over the dice. "I'll give them to the little Kearney. I dare say they were the poor boy's playthings."

The appearance of these relics of wild dissipation, however, had lifted Christie out of her sublime resignation. "For Heaven's sake, Jessie," she said, "look around and see if there is anything more!"

To make sure, they each began to scrimmage; the broken-spirited Christie exhibiting both alacrity and penetration in searching obscure corners. In the dining-room, behind the dresser, three or four books were discovered: an odd volume of Thackeray, another of Dickens, a memorandum-book or diary. "This seems to be Latin," said Jessie, fishing out a smaller book. "I can't read it."

"It's just as well you shouldn't," said Christie shortly, whose ideas of a general classical impropriety had been gathered from the pages of Lemprière's dictionary. "Put it back directly."

Jessie returned certain odes of one Horatius Flaccus to the corner, and uttered an exclamation. "Oh, Christie! here are some letters tied up with a ribbon."

They were two or three prettily written

letters, exhaling a faint odor of refinement and of the pressed flowers that peeped from between the loose leaves. " I see, ' My darling Fairfax.' It's from some woman."

" I don't think much of her, whosoever she is," said Christie, tossing the intact packet back into the corner.

" Nor I," echoed Jessie.

Nevertheless, by some feminine inconsistency, evidently the circumstance did make them think more of *him*, for a minute later, when they had reëntered their own room, Christie remarked, " The idea of petting a man by his family name! Think of mamma ever having called papa ' darling Carr ' ! "

" Oh, but his family name is n't Fairfax," said Jessie hastily; " that's his *first* name, his Christian name. I forget what's his other name, but nobody ever calls him by it."

" Do you mean," said Christie, with glistening eyes and awful deliberation — " do you mean to say that we're expected to fall in with this insufferable familiarity? I suppose they'll be calling *us* by our Christian names next."

"Oh, but they do!" said Jessie, mischievously.

"What!"

"They call me Miss Jessie; and Kearney, the little one, asked me if Christie played."

"And what did you say?"

"I said that you did," answered Jessie, with an affectation of cherubic simplicity. "You do, dear; don't you? . . . There, don't get angry, darling; I could n't flare up all of a sudden in the face of that poor little creature; he looked so absurd — and so — so honest."

Christie turned away, relapsing into her old resigned manner, and assuming her household duties in a quiet, temporizing way that was, however, without hope or expectation.

Mr. Carr, who had dined with his friends under the excuse of not adding to the awkwardness of the first day's housekeeping, returned late at night with a mass of papers and drawings, into which he afterwards withdrew, but not until he had delivered himself of a mysterious package entrusted to him by the young men for his daughters. It contained a contribution to their board in the shape of a silver spoon and battered silver mug, which Jessie chose to facetiously consider as an affecting reminiscence of the youthful Kearney's christening days — which it probably was.

The young girls retired early to their white snowdrifts: Jessie not without some hilarious struggles with hers, in which she was, however, quickly surprised by the deep and refreshing sleep of youth; Christie to lie awake and listen to the night wind, that had changed from the first cool whispers of sunset to the sturdy breath of the mountain. At times the frail house shook and trembled. Wandering gusts laden with the deep resinous odors of the wood found their way through the imperfect jointure of the two cabins, swept her cheek and even stirred her long, wide-open lashes. A broken spray of pine needles rustled along the roof, or a pine cone dropped with a quick reverberating tap-tap that for an instant startled her. Lying thus, wide awake, she fell into a dreamy reminiscence of the past, hearing snatches of old melody in the moving pines, fragments of sentences, old words, and familiar epithets in the murmuring wind at her ear, and even the faint breath of long-forgotten kisses on her cheek. She remembered her mother — a pallid creature, who had slowly faded out of one of her father's vague speculations in a vaguer speculation of her own, beyond his ken — whose place she had promised to take at her father's side. The words, " Watch over him, Christie; he needs a woman's care," again echoed in her ears, as if borne on the night wind from the lonely grave in the lonelier cemetery by the distant sea. She had devoted herself to him with some little sacrifices of self, only remembered now for their uselessness in saving her father the disappointment that sprang from his sanguine and one-idea'd temperament. She thought of him lying asleep in the other room, ready on the morrow to devote those fateful qualities to the new enterprise, that with equally fateful disposition she believed would end in failure. It did not occur to her that the doubts of her own practical nature were almost as dangerous and illogical as his enthusiasm, and that for that reason she was fast losing what little influence she possessed over him. With the example of her mother's weakness before her eyes, she had become an unsparing and distrustful critic, with the sole effect of awakening his distrust and withdrawing his confidence from her. He was beginning to deceive her as he had never deceived her mother. Even Jessie knew more of this last enterprise than she did herself.

All that did not tend to decrease her utter restlessness. It was already past midnight when she noticed that the wind had again abated. The mountain breeze had by this time possessed the stifling valleys and heated bars of the river in its strong, cold embraces; the equilibrium of Nature was restored, and a shadowy mist rose from the hollow. A stillness, more oppressive and intolerable than the previous commotion, began to pervade the house and the surrounding woods. She could hear the regular breathing of the sleepers; she even fancied she could detect the faint pulses of the more distant life in the settlement. The far-off barking of a dog, a lost shout, the indistinct murmur of some nearer watercourse — mere phantoms of sound — made the silence more irritating. With a sudden resolution she arose, dressed herself quietly and completely, threw a heavy cloak over her head and shoulders, and opened the door between the living-room and her own. Her father was sleeping soundly in his bunk in the corner. She passed noiselessly through the room, opened the lightly fastened door, and stepped out into the night.

In the irritation and disgust of her walk hither, she had never noticed the situation of the cabin, as it nestled on the slope at the fringe of the woods; in the preoccupation of her disappointment and the mechanical putting away of her things, she had never looked once from the window of her room, or glanced backward out of the door that she had entered. The view before her was a revelation — a reproach, a surprise that took away her breath. Over her shoulders the newly risen moon poured a flood of silvery light, stretching from her feet across the shining bars of the river to the opposite bank, and on up to the very crest of the Devil's Spur — no longer a huge bulk of crushing shadow, but the steady exaltation of plateau, spur, and terrace clothed with replete and unutterable beauty. In this magical light that beauty seemed to be sustained and carried along by the river winding at its base, lifted again to the broad shoulder of the mountain, and lost only in the distant vista of death-like, overcrowning snow. Behind and above where she stood the towering woods seemed to be waiting with opened ranks to absorb her with the little cabin she had quitted, dwarfed into insignificance in the vast prospect; but nowhere was there another sign or indication of human life and habitation. She looked in vain for the settlement, for the rugged ditches, the scattered cabins, and the unsightly heaps of gravel. In the glamour of the moonlight they had vanished; a veil of silver-gray vapor touched here and there with ebony shadows masked its site. A black strip beyond was the river bank. All else was changed. With a sudden sense of awe and loneliness she turned to the cabin and its sleeping inmates — all that seemed left to her in the vast and stupendous domination of rock and wood and sky.

But in another moment the loneliness passed. A new and delicious sense of an infinite hospitality and friendliness in their silent presence began to possess her. This same slighted, forgotten, uncomprehended, but still foolish and forgiving Nature seemed to be bending over her frightened and listening ear with vague but thrilling murmurings of freedom and independence. She felt her heart expand with its wholesome breath, her soul fill with its sustaining truth. She felt —

What was that?

An unmistakable outburst of a drunken song at the foot of the slope: —

"Oh, my name it is Johnny from Pike,
I'm h—ll on a spree or a strike" . . .

She stopped as crimson with shame and indignation as if the viewless singer had risen before her.

"I knew when to bet, and get up and get" —

"Hush! D—n it all. Don't you hear?"

There was the sound of hurried whispers, a "No" and "Yes," and then a dead silence.

Christie crept nearer to the edge of the slope in the shadow of a buckeye. In the clearer view she could distinguish a staggering figure in the trail below who had evidently been stopped by two other expostulating shadows that were approaching from the shelter of a tree.

"Sho! — did n't know!"

The staggering figure endeavored to straighten itself, and then slouched away in the direction of the settlement. The two mysterious shadows retreated again to the tree, and were lost in its deeper shadow. Christie darted back to the cabin, and softly reëntered her room.

"I thought I heard a noise that woke me,

and I missed you," said Jessie, rubbing her eyes. " Did you see anything ? "

" No," said Christie, beginning to undress.

" You were n't frightened, dear ? "

" Not in the least," said Christie, with a strange little laugh. " Go to sleep."

CHAPTER III.

THE five impulsive millionaires of Devil's Ford fulfilled not a few of their most extravagant promises. In less than six weeks Mr. Carr and his daughters were installed in a new house, built near the site of the double cabin, which was again transferred to the settlement, in order to give greater seclusion to the fair guests. It was a long, roomy, one-storied villa, with a not unpicturesque combination of deep veranda and trellis work, which relieved the flat monotony of the interior and the barrenness of the freshly-cleared ground. An upright piano, brought from Sacramento, occupied the corner of the parlor. A suite of gorgeous furniture, whose pronounced and extravagant glories the young girls instinctively hid under home-made linen covers, had also been spoils from afar. Elsewhere the house was filled with ornaments and decorations that in their incongruity forcibly recalled the gilded plate-glass mirrors of the bedroom in the old cabin. In the hasty furnishing of this Aladdin's palace, the slaves of the ring had evidently seized upon anything that would add to its glory, without reference always to fitness.

"I wish it didn't look so cussedly like a robber's cave," said George Kearney, when they were taking a quiet preliminary survey of the unclassified treasures, before the Carrs took possession.

"Or a gambling hell," said his brother reflectively.

"It's about the same thing, I reckon," said Dick Mattingly, who was supposed, in his fiery youth, to have encountered the similarity.

Nevertheless, the two girls managed to bestow the heterogeneous collection with tasteful adaptation to their needs. A crystal chandelier, which had once lent a fascinating illusion to the game of *Monte*, hung unlighted in the broad hall, where a few other *bizarre* and public articles were relegated. A long red sofa or bench, which had done duty beside a billiard-table found a place here also. Indeed, it is to be feared that some of the more rustic and bashful youths of Devil's Ford, who had felt it incumbent upon them to pay their respects to the new-comers, were more at ease in this vestibule than in the arcana beyond, whose glories they could see through the open door. To others, it represented a recognized state of probation before their *re-entrée* into civilization again. "I reckon, if you don't mind, miss," said the spokesman of one party, "ez this is our first call, we'll sorter hang out in the hall yer, until you'r used to us." On another occasion, one Whiskey Dick, impelled by a sense of duty, paid a visit to the new house and its fair occupants, in a fashion frankly recounted by him afterwards at the bar of the Tecumseh Saloon.

"You see, boys, I dropped in there the other night, when some of you fellows was doin' the high-toned 'thankee, marm' business in the parlor. I just came to anchor in the corner of the sofy in the hall, without lettin' on to say that I was there, and took up a Webster's dictionary that was on the table and laid it open — keerless like, on my knees, ez if I was sorter consultin' it — and kinder dozed off there, listenin' to you fellows gassin' with the young ladies, and that yer Miss Christie just snakin' music outer that pianner, and I reckon I fell asleep. Anyhow, I was there nigh on to two hours. It's mighty soothin', them fashionable calls; sorter knocks the old camp dust outer a fellow, and sets him up again."

It would have been well if the new life of the Devil's Ford had shown no other irregularity than the harmless eccentricities of its original locators. But the news of its sudden fortune, magnified by report, began presently to flood the settlement with another class of adventurers. A tide of waifs, strays, and malcontents of old camps along the river began to set towards Devil's Ford, in very much the same fashion as the *débris*, drift, and alluvium had been carried down in bygone days and cast upon its banks. A few immigrant wagons, diverted from the highways of travel by the fame of the new diggings, halted upon the slopes of Devil's Spur and on the arid flats of the Ford, and disgorged their sallow freight of alkali-poisoned, prematurely-aged women and children and maimed and fever-stricken men. Against this rude form of domesticity were opposed the chromo-tinted dresses and extravagant complexions of a few single unattended women — happily seen more often at night and behind gilded bars than in the garish light of day — and an equal number of pale-faced, dark-moustached, well-dressed, and suspiciously idle men. A dozen rivals of Thompson's Saloon had sprung up along the narrow main street. There were two new hotels — one a " Temperance House," whose ascetic quality was confined only to the abnegation of whiskey — a rival stage office, and a small one-storied building, from which the " Sierran Banner " fluttered weekly, for " ten dollars a year, in advance." Insufferable in the glare of a Sabbath sun, bleak, windy, and flaring in the gloom of a Sabbath night, and hopelessly depressing on all days of the week, the First Presbyterian

Church lifted its blunt steeple from the barrenest area of the flats, and was hideous! The civic improvements so enthusiastically contemplated by the five millionaires in the earlier pages of this veracious chronicle — the fountain, reservoir, town-hall, and free library — had not yet been erected. Their sites had been anticipated by more urgent buildings and mining works, unfortunately not considered in the sanguine dreams of the enthusiasts, and, more significant still, their cost and expense had been also anticipated by the enormous outlay of their earnings in the work upon Devil's Ditch.

Nevertheless, the liberal fulfilment of their promise in the new house in the suburbs blinded the young girls' eyes to their shortcomings in the town. Their own remoteness and elevation above its feverish life kept them from the knowledge of much that was strange, and perhaps disturbing to their equanimity. As they did not mix with the immigrant women — Miss Jessie's good-natured intrusion into one of their half-nomadic camps one day having been met with rudeness and suspicion — they gradually fell into the way of trusting the responsibility of new acquaintances to the hands of their original hosts, and of consulting them in the matter of local recreation. It thus occurred that one day the two girls, on their way to the main street for an hour's shopping at the Ville de Paris and Variety Store, were stopped by Dick Mattingly a few yards from their house, with the remark that, as the county election was then in progress, it would be advisable for them to defer their intention for a few hours. As he did not deem it necessary to add that two citizens, in the exercise of a freeman's franchise, had been supplementing their ballots with bullets, in front of an admiring crowd, they knew nothing of the accident that removed from Devil's Ford an entertaining stranger, who had only the night before partaken of their hospitality.

A week or two later, returning one morning from a stroll in the forest, Christie and Jessie were waylaid by George Kearney and Fairfax, and, under pretext of being shown a new and romantic trail, were diverted from the regular path. This enabled Mattingly and Maryland Joe to cut down the body of a man hanged by the Vigilance Committee a few hours before on the regular trail, and to remonstrate with the committee on the incompatibility of such exhibitions with a maidenly worship of nature.

"With the whole county to hang a man in," expostulated Joe, "you might keep clear of Carr's woods."

It is needless to add that the young girls never knew of this act of violence, or the delicacy that kept them in ignorance of it. Mr. Carr was too absorbed in business to give heed to what he looked upon as a convulsion of society as natural as a geological upheaval, and too prudent to provoke the criticism of his daughters by comment in their presence.

An equally unexpected confidence, however, took its place. Mr. Carr having finished his coffee one morning, lingered a moment over his perfunctory paternal embraces, with the awkwardness of a preoccupied man endeavoring by the assumption of a lighter interest to veil another abstraction.

"And what are we doing to-day, Christie?" he asked, as Jessie left the dining-room.

"Oh, pretty much the usual thing — nothing in particular. If George Kearney gets the horses from the summit, we're going to ride over to Indian Spring to picnic. Fairfax — Mr. Munroe — I always forget that man's real name in this dreadfully familiar country — well, he's coming to escort us, and take me, I suppose — that is, if Kearney takes Jessie."

"A very nice arrangement," returned her father, with a slight nervous contraction of the corners of his mouth and eyelids to indicate mischievousness. "I've no doubt they'll both be here. You know they usually are — ha! ha! And what about the two Mattinglys and Philip Kearney, eh?" he continued; "won't they be jealous?"

"It isn't their turn," said Christie carelessly; "besides, they'll probably be there."

"And I suppose they're beginning to be resigned," said Carr, smiling.

"What on earth are you talking of, father?"

She turned her clear brown eyes upon him, and was regarding him with such manifest unconsciousness of the drift of his speech, and, withal, a little vague impatience of his archness, that Mr. Carr was feebly alarmed. It had the effect of banishing his assumed playfulness, which made his serious explanation the more irritating.

"Well, I rather thought that — that young Kearney was paying considerable attention to — to — to Jessie," replied her father, with hesitating gravity.

"What! that boy?"

"Young Kearney is one of the original locators, and an equal partner in the mine. A very enterprising young fellow. In fact, much more advanced and bolder in his conceptions than the others. I find no difficulty with him."

At another time Christie would have questioned the convincing quality of this proof, but she was too much shocked at her father's first suggestion, to think of anything else.

"You don't mean to say, father, that you are talking seriously of these men — your friends — whom we see every day — and our only company?"

"No, no!" said Mr. Carr hastily; "you misunderstand. I don't suppose that Jessie or you" —

"Or *me!* Am *I* included?"

"You don't let me speak, Christie. I mean, I am not talking seriously," continued Mr. Carr, with his most serious aspect, "of you and Jessie in this matter; but it may be a serious thing to these young men to be thrown continually in the company of two attractive girls."

"I understand — you mean that we should not see so much of them," said Christie, with a frank expression of relief so genuine as to utterly discompose her father. "Perhaps you are right, though I fail to discover anything serious in the attentions of young Kearney to Jessie — or — whoever it may be — to me. But it will be very easy to remedy it, and see less of them. Indeed, we might begin to-day with some excuse."

"Yes — certainly. Of course!" said Mr. Carr, fully convinced of his utter failure, but, like most weak creatures, consoling himself with the reflection that he had not shown his hand or committed himself. "Yes; but it would perhaps be just as well for the present to let things go on as they were. We'll talk of it again — I'm in a hurry now," and, edging himself through the door, he slipped away.

"What do you think is father's last idea?" said Christie, with, I fear, a slight lack of reverence in her tone, as her sister reëntered the room. "He thinks George Kearney is paying you too much attention."

"No!" said Jessie, replying to her sister's half-interrogative, half-amused glance with a frank, unconscious smile.

"Yes, and he says that Fairfax — I think it's Fairfax — is equally fascinated with *me*."

Jessie's brow slightly contracted as she looked curiously at her sister.

"Of all things," she said, "I wonder if any one has put that idea into his dear old head. He could n't have thought it himself."

"I don't know," said Christie musingly; "but perhaps it 's just as well if we kept a little more to ourselves for a while."

"Did father say so?" said Jessie quickly.

"No, but that is evidently what he meant."

"Ye-es," said Jessie slowly, "unless" —

"Unless what?" said Christie sharply. "Jessie, you don't for a moment mean to say that you could possibly conceive of anything else?"

"I mean to say," said Jessie, stealing her arm around her sister's waist demurely, "that you are perfectly right. We'll keep away from these fascinating Devil's Forders, and particularly the youngest Kearney. I believe there has been some ill-natured gossip. I remember that the other day, when we passed the shanty of that Pike County family on the slope, there were three women at the door, and one of them said something that made poor little Kearney turn white and pink alternately, and dance with suppressed rage. I suppose the old lady — M'Corkle, that's her name — would like to have a share of our cavaliers for her Euphemy and Mamie. I dare say it's only right; I would lend them the cherub occasionally, and you might let them have Mr. Munroe twice a week."

She laughed, but her eyes sought her sister's with a certain watchfulness of expression.

Christie shrugged her shoulders, with a suggestion of disgust.

"Don't joke. We ought to have thought of all this before."

"But when we first knew them, in the dear old cabin, there wasn't any other woman and nobody to gossip, and that's what made it so nice. I don't think so very much of civilization, do you?" said the young lady pertly.

Christie did not reply. Perhaps she was thinking the same thing. It certainly had been very pleasant to enjoy the spontaneous and chivalrous homage of these men, with no further suggestion of recompense or responsibility than the permission to be worshipped; but beyond that she racked her brain in vain to recall any look or act that proclaimed the lover. These men, whom she had found so relapsed into barbarism that they had forgotten the most ordinary forms of civilization; these men, even in whose extravagant admiration there was a certain loss of self-respect, that as a woman she would never forgive; these men, who seemed to belong to another race — impossible! Yet it was so.

"What construction must they have put upon her father's acceptance of their presents — of their company — of her freedom in their presence? No! they must have understood from the beginning that she and her sister had never looked upon them except as transient hosts and chance acquaintances. Any other idea was preposterous. And yet"—

It was the recurrence of this "yet" that alarmed her. For she remembered now that but for their slavish devotion they might claim to be her equal. According to her father's account, they had come from homes as good as their own; they were certainly more than her equal in fortune; and her father had come to them as an employé, until they had taken him into partnership. If there had only been sentiment of any kind connected with any of them! But they were all alike, brave, unselfish, humorous — and often ridiculous. If anything, Dick Mattingly was funniest by nature, and made her laugh more. Maryland Joe, his brother, told better stories (sometimes of Dick), though not so good a mimic as the other Kearney, who had a fairly sympathetic voice in singing. They were all good-looking enough; perhaps they set store on that — men are so vain!

And as for her own rejected suitor, Fairfax Munroe, except for a kind of grave and proper motherliness about his protecting manner, he absolutely was the most indistinctive of them all. He had once brought her some rare tea from the Chinese camp, and had taught her how to make it; he had cautioned her against sitting under the trees at nightfall; he had once taken off his coat to wrap around her. Really, if this were the only evidence of devotion that could be shown, she was safe!

"Well," said Jessie, "it amuses you, I see."

Christie checked the smile that had been dimpling the cheek nearest Jessie, and turned upon her the face of an elder sister.

"Tell me, have *you* noticed this extraordinary attention of Mr. Munroe to me?"

"Candidly?" asked Jessie, seating herself comfortably on the table sideways, and endeavoring to pull her skirt over her little feet. "Honest Injun?"

"Don't be idiotic, and, above all, don't be slangy! Of course, candidly."

"Well, no. I can't say that I have."

"Then," said Christie, "why in the name of all that's preposterous, do they persist in pairing me off with the least interesting man of the lot?"

Jessie leaped from the table.

"Come now," she said, with a little nervous laugh, "he's not so bad as all that. You don't know him. But what does it matter now, as long as we're not going to see them any more?"

"They're coming here for the ride to-day," said Christie resignedly. "Father thought it better not to break it off at once."

"Father thought so!" echoed Jessie, stopping, with her hand on the door.

"Yes; why do you ask?"

But Jessie had already left the room, and was singing in the hall.

CHAPTER IV.

THE afternoon did not, however, bring their expected visitors. It brought, instead, a brief note by the hands of Whiskey Dick from Fairfax, apologizing for some business that kept him and George Kearney from accompanying the ladies. It added that the horses were at the disposal of themselves and any escort they might select, if they would kindly give the message to Whiskey Dick.

The two girls looked at each other awkwardly; Jessie did not attempt to conceal a slight pout.

"It looks as if they were anticipating us," she said, with a half-forced smile. "I wonder, now, if there really has been any gossip? But no! They would n't have stopped for that, unless" — She looked curiously at her sister.

"Unless what?" repeated Christie; "you are horribly mysterious this morning."

"Am I? It's nothing. But they're wanting an answer. Of course you'll decline."

"And intimate we only care for their company! No! We'll say we're sorry they can't come, and — accept their horses. We can do without an escort, we two."

"Capital!" said Jessie, clapping her hands. "We'll show them" —

"We'll show them nothing," interrupted Christie decidedly. "In our place there's only the one thing to do. Where is this — Whiskey Dick?"

"In the parlor."

"The parlor!" echoed Christie. "Whiskey Dick? What — is he" —

"Yes; he's all right," said Jessie confidently. "He's been here before, but he stayed in the hall; he was so shy. I don't think you saw him."

"I should think not — Whiskey Dick!"

"Oh, you can call him Mr. Hall, if you like," said Jessie, laughing. "His real name is Dick Hall. If you want to be funny, you can say Alky Hall, as the others do."

Christie's only reply to this levity was a look of superior resignation as she crossed the hall and entered the parlor.

Then ensued one of those surprising, mystifying, and utterly inexplicable changes that leave the masculine being so helpless in the hands of his feminine master. Before Christie opened the door her face underwent a rapid transformation: the gentle glow of a refined woman's welcome suddenly beamed in her interested eyes; the impulsive courtesy of an expectant hostess eagerly seizing a long-looked-for opportunity broke in a smile upon her lips as she swept across the room, and stopped with her two white outstretched hands before Whiskey Dick.

It needed only the extravagant contrast presented by that gentleman to complete the tableau. Attired in a suit of shining black alpaca, the visitor had evidently prepared himself with some care for a possible interview. He was seated by the French window opening upon the veranda, as if to secure a retreat in case of an emergency. Scrupulously washed and shaven, some of the soap appeared to have lingered in his eyes and inflamed the lids, even while it lent a sleek and shining lustre, not unlike his coat, to his smooth black hair. Nevertheless, leaning back in his chair, he had allowed a large white handkerchief to depend gracefully from his fingers — a pose at once suggesting easy and elegant languor.

"How kind of you to give me an opportunity to make up for my misfortune when you last called! I was so sorry to have missed you. But it was entirely my fault! You were hurried, I think — you conversed with others in the hall — you" —

She stopped to assist him to pick up the handkerchief that had fallen, and the Panama hat that had rolled from his lap towards the window when he had started suddenly to his feet at the apparition of grace and beauty. As he still nervously retained the two hands he had grasped, this would have been a difficult feat, even had he not endeavored at the same moment, by a backward furtive kick, to propel the hat out of the window, at which she laughingly broke from his grasp and flew to the rescue.

"Don't mind it, miss," he said hurriedly. "It is not worth your demeaning yourself to touch it. Leave it outside thar, miss. I wouldn't have toted it in, anyhow, if some of those high falutin' fellows hadn't allowed, the other night, ez it were the reg'lar thing to do; as if, miss, any gentleman kalkilated to ever put on his hat in the house afore a lady!"

But Christie had already possessed herself of the unlucky object, and had placed it upon the table. This compelled Whiskey Dick to rise again, and as an act of careless good breeding to drop his handkerchief in it. He then leaned one elbow upon the piano, and, crossing one foot over the other, remained standing in an attitude he remembered to have seen in the pages of an illustrated paper as portraying the hero in some drawing-room scene. It was easy and effective, but seemed to be more favorable to revery than conversation. Indeed, he remembered that he had forgotten to consult the letterpress as to which it represented.

"I see you agree with me, that politeness

is quite a matter of intention," said Christie, "and not of mere fashion and rules. Now, for instance," she continued, with a dazzling smile, " I suppose, according to the rules, I ought to give you a note to Mr. Munroe, accepting his offer. That is all that is required; but it seems so much nicer, don't you think, to tell it to *you* for *him*, and have the pleasure of your company and a little chat at the same time."

"That's it, that's just it, Miss Carr; you've hit it in the centre this time," said Whiskey Dick, now quite convinced that his attitude was not intended for eloquence, and shifting back to his own seat, hat and all; "that's tantamount to what I said to the boys just now. 'You want an excuse,' sez I, 'for not goin' out with the young ladies. So, accorden' to rules, you writes a letter allowin' buzziness and that sorter thing detains you. But wot's the facts? You're a gentleman, and as gentlemen you and George comes to the opinion that you're rather playin' it for all it's worth in this yer house, you know — comin' here night and day, off and on, reg'lar sociable and fam'ly like, and makin' people talk about things they ain't any call to talk about, and, what's a darned sight more, *you fellows* ain't got any right *yet* to allow 'em to talk about, d' ye see?'" He paused, out of breath.

It was Miss Christie's turn to move about. In changing her seat to the piano-stool, so as to be nearer her visitor, she brushed down some loose music, which Whiskey Dick hastened to pick up.

"Pray don't mind it," she said, "pray don't, really — let it be" — But Whiskey Dick, feeling himself on safe ground in this attention, persisted to the bitter end of a disintegrated and well-worn "Trovatore." "So that is what Mr. Munroe said," she remarked quietly.

"Not just then, in course, but it's what's bin on his mind and in his talk for days off and on," returned Dick, with a knowing smile and a nod of mysterious confidence. "Bless your soul, Miss Carr, folks like you and me don't need to have them things explained. That's what I said to him, sez I.

'Don't send no note, but just go up there and hev it out fair and square, and say what you do mean.' But they would hev the note, and I kalkilated to bring it. But when I set my eyes on you, and heard you express yourself as you did just now, I sez to myself, sez I, 'Dick, yer's a young lady, and a fash'nable lady at that, ez don't go foolin' round on rules and etiketts' — excuse my freedom, Miss Carr — 'and you and her,' sez I, 'kin just discuss this yer matter in a sociable, off-hand, fash'nable way.' They 're a good lot o' boys, Miss Carr, a square lot — white men all of 'em; but they 're a little soft and green, may be, from livin' in these yer pine woods along o' the other sap. They just worship the ground you and your sister tread on — certain! of course! of course!" he added hurriedly, recognizing Christie's half-conscious, deprecating gesture with more exaggerated deprecation. "I understand. But what I wanter say is that they 'd be willin' to be that ground, and lie down and let you walk over them — so to speak, Miss Carr, so to speak — if it would keep the hem

of your gown from gettin' soiled in the mud
o' the camp. But it would n't do for them
to make a reg'lar curderoy road o' themselves for the huol camp to trapse over, on
the mere chance of your some time passin'
that way, would it now?"

"Won't you let me offer you some re-
freshment, Mr. Hall?" said Christie, rising,
with a slight color. "I 'm really ashamed
of my forgetfulness again, but I 'm afraid
it 's partly *your* fault for entertaining me to
the exclusion of yourself. No, thank you,
let me fetch it for you."

She turned to a handsome sideboard near
the door, and presently faced him again with
a decanter of whiskey and a glass in her
hand, and a return of the bewitching smile
she had worn on entering.

"But perhaps you don't take whiskey?"
suggested the arch deceiver, with a sudden
affected but pretty perplexity of eye, brow,
and lips.

For the first time in his life Whiskey
Dick hesitated between two forms of in-
toxication. But he was still nervous and

uneasy; habit triumphed, and he took the whiskey. He, however, wiped his lips with a slight wave of his handkerchief, to support a certain easy elegance which he firmly believed relieved the act of any vulgar quality.

"Yes, ma'am," he continued, after an exhilarated pause. "Ez I said afore, this yer's a matter you and me kin discuss after the fashion o' society. My idea is that these yer boys should kinder let up on you and Miss Jessie for a while, and do a little more permiskus attention round the Ford. There's one or two families yer with grown-up gals ez oughter be squared; that is — the boys mighter put in a few fancy touches among them — kinder take 'em buggy riding — or to church — once in a while — just to take the pizen outer their tongues, and make a kind o' bluff to the parents, d'ye see? That would sorter divert their own minds; and even if it did n't, it would kinder get 'em accustomed agin to the old style and their own kind. I want to warn ye agin an idea that might occur to you in a giniral way. I don't say you hev the idea, but it's kind o' nat'ral you might be thinkin' of it some time, and I thought I'd warn you agin it."

"I think we understand each other too well to differ much, Mr. Hall," said Christie, still smiling; "but what is the idea?"

The delicate compliment to their confidential relations and the slight stimulus of liquor had tremulously exalted Whiskey Dick. Affecting to look cautiously out of the window and around the room, he ventured to draw nearer the young woman with a half-paternal, half-timid familiarity.

"It might have occurred to you," he said, laying his hand lightly, holding his handkerchief as if to veil mere vulgar contact, on Christie's shoulder, "that it would be a good thing on *your* side to invite down some of your high-toned gentlemen friends from 'Frisco to visit you and escort you round. It seems quite nat'ral like, and I don't say it ain't, but — the boys wouldn't stand it."

In spite of her self-possession, Christie's eyes suddenly darkened, and she involuntarily drew herself up. But Whiskey Dick, guiltily attributing the movement to his own indiscreet gesture, said, "Excuse me, miss," recovered himself by lightly dusting her shoulder with his handkerchief, as if to remove the impression, and her smile returned.

"They would n't stand it," said Dick, "and there 'd be some shooting! Not afore you, miss — not afore you, in course! But they 'd adjourn to the woods some morning with them city folks, and hev it out with rifles at a hundred yards. Or, seein' ez they 're city folks, the boys would do the square thing with pistols at twelve paces. They 're good boys, as I said afore; but they 're quick and tetchy — George, being the youngest, nat'rally is the tetchiest. You know how it is, Miss Carr; his pretty, gal-like face and little moustaches haz cost him half a dozen scrimmages already. He 'z had a fight for every hair that 's growed in his moustache since he kem here."

"Say no more, Mr. Hall!" said Christie, rising and pressing her hands lightly on Dick's tremulous fingers. "If I ever had any such idea, I should abandon it now;

you are quite right in this as in your other opinions. I shall never cease to be thankful to Mr. Munroe and Mr. Kearney that they intrusted this delicate matter to your hands."

"Well," said the gratified and reddening visitor, " it ain't perhaps the square thing to them or myself to say that they reckoned to have me discuss their delicate affairs for them, but "—

" I understand," interrupted Christie. "They simply gave you the letter as a friend. It was my good fortune to find you a sympathizing and liberal man of the world." The delighted Dick, with conscious vanity beaming from every feature of his shining face, lightly waved the compliment aside with his handkerchief, as she continued, " But I am forgetting the message. We accept the horses. Of course we *could* do without an escort; but, forgive my speaking so frankly, are *you* engaged this afternoon ? "

" Excuse me, miss, I don't take " — stammered Dick, scarcely believing his ears.

"Could you give us your company as an escort?" repeated Christie, with a smile.

Was he awake or dreaming, or was this some trick of liquor in his often distorted fancy? He, Whiskey Dick! the butt of his friends, the chartered oracle of the bar-rooms, even in whose wretched vanity there was always the haunting suspicion that he was despised and scorned; he, who had dared so much in speech, and achieved so little in fact! he, whose habitual weakness had even led him into the wildest indiscretion here; he — now offered a reward for that indiscretion! He, Whiskey Dick, the solicited escort of these two beautiful and peerless girls! What would they say at the Ford? What would his friends think? It would be all over the Ford the next day. His past would be vindicated, his future secured. He grew erect at the thought. It was almost in other voice, and with no trace of his previous exaggeration, that he said, "With pleasure."

"Then, if you will bring the horses at once, we shall be ready when you return."

In another instant he had vanished, as if afraid to trust the reality of his good fortune to the dangers of delay. At the end of half an hour he reappeared, leading the two horses, himself mounted on a half-broken mustang. A pair of large, jingling silver spurs and a stiff *sombrero*, borrowed with the mustang from some mysterious source, were donned to do honor to the occasion.

The young girls were not yet ready, but he was shown by the Chinese servant into the parlor to wait for them. The decanter of whiskey and glasses were still invitingly there. He was hot, trembling, and flushed with triumph. He walked to the table and laid his hand on the decanter, when an odd thought flashed upon him. He would not drink this time. No, it should not be said that he, the selected escort of the *élite* of Devil's Ford, had to fill himself up with whiskey before they started. The boys might turn to each other in their astonishment, as he proudly passed with his fair companions, and say, "It's Whiskey Dick," but he'd be d——d if they should add, "and full as ever." No, sir! Nor when he was riding beside these real ladies, and leaning over them at some confidential moment, should they even know it from his breath! No. . . . Yet a thimbleful, taken straight, only a thimbleful, wouldn't be much, and might help to pull him together. He again reached his trembling hand for the decanter, hesitated, and then, turning his back upon it, resolutely walked to the open window. Almost at the same instant he found himself face to face with Christie on the veranda.

She looked into his bloodshot eyes, and cast a swift glance at the decanter.

"Won't you take something before you go?" she said sweetly.

"I — reckon — not, jest now," stammered Whiskey Dick, with a heroic effort.

"You're right," said Christie. "I see you are like me. It's too hot for anything fiery. Come with me."

She led him to the dining-room, and pouring out a glass of iced tea handed it to him. Poor Dick was not prepared for this terrible culmination. Whiskey Dick and iced tea!

But under pretence of seeing if it was properly flavored, Christie raised it to her own lips.

"Try it, to please me."

He drained the goblet.

"Now, then," said Christie gayly, "let's find Jessie, and be off!"

CHAPTER V.

WHATEVER might have been his other deficiencies as an escort, Whiskey Dick was a good horseman, and, in spite of his fractious brute, exhibited such skill and confidence as to at once satisfy the young girls of his value to them in the management of their own horses, to whom side-saddles were still an alarming novelty. Jessie, who had probably already learned from her sister the purport of Dick's confidences, had received him with equal cordiality and perhaps a more unqualified amusement; and now, when fairly lifted into the saddle by his tremulous but respectful hands, made a very charming picture of youthful and rosy satisfaction. And when Christie, more fascinating than ever in her riding-habit, took her place on the other side of Dick, as they sallied from the gate, that gentleman felt his cup of happiness complete. His triumphal *entrée* into the

world of civilization and fashion was secure.
He did not regret the untasted liquor; here
was an experience in after years to lean his
back against comfortably in bar-rooms, to
entrance or defy mankind. He had even got
so far as to formulate in fancy the sentence:
"I remember, gentlemen, that one afternoon, being on a *pasear* with two fash'nable
young ladies," etc., etc.

At present, however, he was obliged to
confine himself to the functions of an elegant
guide and *cicerone* — when not engaged in
"having it out" with his horse. Their way
lay along the slope, crossing the high-road at
right angles, to reach the deeper woods beyond. Dick would have lingered on the
highway — ostensibly to point out to his
companions the new flume that had taken
the place of the condemned ditch, but really
in the hope of exposing himself in his glory
to the curious eyes of the wayfaring world.
Unhappily the road was deserted in the still
powerful sunlight, and he was obliged to seek
the cover of the woods, with a passing compliment to the parent of his charges. Wav-

ing his hand towards the flume, he said, "Look at that work of your father's; there ain't no other man in Californy but Philip Carr ez would hev the grit to hold up such a bluff agin natur and agin luck ez that yer flume stands for. I don't say it 'cause you 're his daughters, ladies! That ain't the style, ez *you* know, in sassiety, Miss Carr," he added, turning to Christie as the more socially experienced. "No! but there ain't another man to be found ez could do it. It cost already two hundred thousand; it 'll cost five hundred thousand afore it 's done; and every cent of it is got out of the yearth beneath it, or *hez got* to be out of it. 'Tain't ev'ry man, Miss Carr, ez hev got the pluck to pledge not only what he 's got, but what he reckons to git."

"But suppose he don't get it?" said Christie, slightly contracting her brows.

"Then there 's the flume to show for it," said Dick.

"But of what use is the flume, if there is n't any more gold?" continued Christie, almost angrily.

"That's good from *you*, miss," said Dick, giving way to a fit of hilarity. "That's good for a fash'nable young lady — own daughter of Philip Carr. She sez, says she," continued Dick, appealing to the sedate pines for appreciation of Christie's rare humor, "'Wot's the use of a flume, when gold ain't there?' I must tell that to the boys."

"And what's the use of the gold in the ground when the flume isn't there to work it out?" said Jessie to her sister, with a cautioning glance towards Dick.

But Dick did not notice the look that passed between the sisters. The richer humor of Jessie's retort had thrown him into convulsions of laughter.

"And now *she* says, wot's the use o' the gold without the flume? 'Xcuse me, ladies, but that's just puttin' the hull question that's agitatin' this yer camp inter two speeches as clear as crystal. There's the hull crowd outside — and some on 'em inside, like Fairfax, hez their doubts — ez says with Miss Christie; and there's all of us inside, ez holds Miss Jessie's views."

"I never heard Mr. Munroe say that the flume was wrong," said Jessie quickly.

"Not to you, nat'rally," said Dick, with a confidential look at Christie; "but I reckon he'd like some of the money it cost laid out for suthin' else. But what's the odds? The gold is there, and *we're* bound to get it."

Dick was the foreman of a gang of paid workmen, who had replaced the millionaires in mere manual labor, and the *we* was a polite figure of speech.

The conversation seemed to have taken an unfortunate turn, and both the girls experienced a feeling of relief when they entered the long gulch or defile that led to Indian Spring. The track now becoming narrow, they were obliged to pass in single file along the precipitous hillside, led by this escort. This effectually precluded any further speech, and Christie at once surrendered herself to the calm, obliterating influences of the forest. The settlement and its gossip were far behind and forgotten. In the absorption of nature, her companions passed out of her mind, even as they sometimes passed out of her sight in the windings of the shadowy trail. As she rode alone, the fronds of breast-high ferns seemed to caress her with outstretched and gently-detaining hands; strange wild-flowers sprang up through the parting underbrush; even the granite rocks that at times pressed closely upon the trail appeared as if cushioned to her contact with star-rayed mosses, or lightly flung after her long lassoes of delicate vines. She recalled the absolute freedom of their *al-fresco* life in the old double cabin, when she spent the greater part of her waking hours under the mute trees in the encompassing solitude, and, half regretting the more civilized restraints of this newer and more ambitious abode, forgot that she had ever rebelled against it. The social complication that threatened her now seemed to her rather the outcome of her half-civilized parlor than of the sylvan glade. How easy it would have been to have kept the cabin, and then to have gone away entirely, than for her father to have allowed them to be compromised with the growing fortunes of the settlement! The suspicions and distrust that she had always felt of their fortunes seemed to grow with the involuntary admission of Whiskey Dick that they were shared by others who were practical men. She was fain to have recourse to the prospect again to banish these thoughts, and this opened her eyes to the fact that her companions had been missing from the trail ahead of her for some time. She quickened her pace slightly to reach a projecting point of rock that gave her a more extended prospect. But they had evidently disappeared.

She was neither alarmed nor annoyed. She could easily overtake them soon, for they would miss her, and return or wait for her at the spring. At the worst she would have no difficulty in retracing her steps home. In her present mood, she could readily spare their company; indeed she was not sorry that no other being should interrupt that sympathy with the free woods which was beginning to possess her.

She was destined, however, to be disappointed. She had not proceeded a hundred yards before she noticed the moving figure of a man beyond her in the hillside chaparral above the trail. He seemed to be going in the same direction as herself, and, as she fancied, endeavoring to avoid her. This excited her curiosity to the point of urging her horse forward until the trail broadened into the level forest again, which she now remembered was a part of the environs of Indian Spring. The stranger hesitated, pausing once or twice with his back towards her, as if engaged in carefully examining the dwarf willows to select a switch. Christie slightly checked her speed as she drew nearer; when, as if obedient to a sudden resolution, he turned and advanced towards her. She was relieved and yet surprised to recognize the boyish face and figure of George Kearney. He was quite pale and agitated, although attempting, by a jaunty swinging of the switch he had just cut, to assume the appearance of ease and confidence.

Here was an opportunity. Christie resolved to profit by it. She did not doubt that the young fellow had already passed her sister on the trail, but, from bashfulness, had not dared to approach her. By inviting his confidence, she would doubtless draw something from him that would deny or corroborate her father's opinion of his sentiments. If he was really in love with Jessie, she would learn what reasons he had for expecting a serious culmination of his suit, and perhaps she might be able delicately to open his eyes to the truth. If, as she believed, it was only a boyish fancy, she would laugh him out of it with that *camaraderie* which had always existed between them. A half motherly sympathy, albeit born quite as much from a contemplation of his beautiful yearning eyes as from his interesting position, lightened the smile with which she greeted him.

"So you contrived to throw over your stupid business and join us, after all," she said; "or was it that you changed your mind at the last moment?" she added mischievously. "I thought only we women were permitted that!" Indeed, she could not help noticing that there was really a strong feminine suggestion in the shifting color and slightly conscious eyelids of the young fellow.

"Do young girls always change their minds?" asked George, with an embarrassed smile.

"Not always; but sometimes they don't know their own mind — particularly if they are very young; and when they do at last, you clever creatures of men, who have interpreted their ignorance to please yourselves, abuse them for being fickle." She stopped to observe the effect of what she believed a rather clear and significant exposition of Jessie's and George's possible situation. But she was not prepared for the look of blank resignation that seemed to drive the color from his face and moisten the fire of his dark eyes.

"I reckon you're right," he said, looking down.

"Oh! we're not accusing you of fickleness," said Christie gayly; "although you didn't come, and we were obliged to ask Mr. Hall to join us. I suppose you found him and Jessie just now?"

But George made no reply. The color was slowly coming back to his face, which, as she glanced covertly at him, seemed to have grown so much older that his returning blood might have brought two or three years with it.

"Really, Mr. Kearney," she said dryly, "one would think that some silly, conceited girl" — she was quite earnest in her epithets, for a sudden, angry conviction of some coquetry and disingenuousness in Jessie had come to her in contemplating its effects upon the young fellow at her side — "some country jilt, had been trying her rustic hand upon you."

"She is not silly, conceited, nor countrified," said George, slowly raising his beautiful eyes to the young girl half reproachfully. "It is I who am all that. No, she is right, and you know it."

Much as Christie admired and valued her sister's charms, she thought this was really going too far. What had Jessie ever done — what was Jessie — to provoke and remain insensible to such a blind devotion as this? And really, looking at him now, he was not so *very young* for Jessie; whether his unfortunate passion had brought out all his latent manliness, or whether he had hitherto kept his serious nature in the background, certainly he was not a boy. And certainly his was not a passion that he could be laughed out of. It was getting very tiresome. She wished she had not met him — at least until she had had some clearer understanding with her sister. He was still walking beside her, with his hand on her bridle rein, partly to lead her horse over some boulders in the trail, and partly to conceal his first embarrassment. When they had fairly reached the woods, he stopped.

"I am going to say good-by, Miss Carr."

"Are you not coming further? We must be near Indian Spring, now; Mr. Hall and — and Jessie — cannot be far away. You will keep me company until we meet them?"

"No," he replied quietly. "I only stopped you to say good-by. I am going away."

"Not from Devil's Ford?" she asked, in

half-incredulous astonishment. " At least, not for long ? "

" I am not coming back," he replied.

" But this is very abrupt," she said hurriedly, feeling that in some ridiculous way she had precipitated an equally ridiculous catastrophe. " Surely you are not going away in this fashion, without saying goodby to Jessie and — and father ? "

" I shall see your father, of course — and you will give my regards to Miss Jessie."

He evidently was in earnest. Was there ever anything so perfectly preposterous ? She became indignant.

" Of course," she said coldly, " I won't detain you ; your business must be urgent, and I forgot — at least I had forgotten until to-day — that you have other duties more important than that of squire of dames. I am afraid this forgetfulness made me think you would not part from us in quite such a business fashion. I presume, if you had not met me just now, we should none of us have seen you again ? "

He did not reply.

"Will you say good-by, Miss Carr?"

He held out his hand.

"One moment, Mr. Kearney. If I have said anything which you think justifies this very abrupt leave-taking, I beg you will forgive and forget it — or, at least, let it have no more weight with you than the idle words of any woman. I only spoke generally. You know — I — I might be mistaken."

His eyes, which had dilated when she began to speak, darkened; his color, which had quickly come, as quickly sank when she had ended.

"Don't say that, Miss Carr. It is not like you, and — it is useless. You know what I meant a moment ago. I read it in your reply. You meant that I, like others, had deceived myself. Did you not?"

She could not meet those honest eyes with less than equal honesty. She knew that Jessie did not love him — would not marry him — whatever coquetry she might have shown.

"I did not mean to offend you," she said hesitatingly; "I only half suspected it when I spoke."

"And you wish to spare me the avowal?" he said bitterly.

"To me, perhaps, yes, by anticipating it. I could not tell what ideas you might have gathered from some indiscreet frankness of Jessie — or my father," she added, with almost equal bitterness.

"I have never spoken to either," he replied quickly. He stopped, and added, after a moment's mortifying reflection, "I've been brought up in the woods, Miss Carr, and I suppose I have followed my feelings, instead of the etiquette of society."

Christie was too relieved at the rehabilitation of Jessie's truthfulness to notice the full significance of his speech.

"Good-by," he said again, holding out his hand.

"Good-by!"

She extended her own, ungloved, with a frank smile. He held it for a moment, with his eyes fixed upon hers. Then suddenly, as if obeying an uncontrollable impulse, he crushed it like a flower again and again against his burning lips, and darted away.

Christie sank back in her saddle with a little cry, half of pain and half of frightened surprise. Had the poor boy suddenly gone mad, or was this vicarious farewell a part of the courtship of Devil's Ford? She looked at her little hand, which had reddened under the pressure, and suddenly felt the flush extending to her cheeks and the roots of her hair. This was intolerable.

"Christie!"

It was her sister emerging from the wood to seek her. In another moment she was at her side.

"We thought you were following," said Jessie. "Good heavens! how you look! What has happened?"

"Nothing. I met Mr. Kearney a moment ago on the trail. He is going away, and — and " — She stopped, furious and flushing.

"And," said Jessie, with a burst of merriment, "he told you at last he loved you. Oh, Christie!"

CHAPTER VI.

THE abrupt departure of George Kearney from Devil's Ford excited but little interest in the community, and was soon forgotten. It was generally attributed to differences between himself and his partners on the question of further outlay of their earnings on mining improvements — he and Philip Carr alone representing a sanguine minority whose faith in the future of the mine accepted any risks. It was alleged by some that he had sold out to his brother; it was believed by others that he had simply gone to Sacramento to borrow money on his share, in order to continue the improvements on his own responsibility. The partners themselves were uncommunicative; even Whiskey Dick, who since his remarkable social elevation had become less oracular, much to his own astonishment, contributed nothing to the gossip except a suggestion that as the fiery temper of George Kearney brooked no opposition, even from his brother, it was better they should separate before the estrangement became serious.

Mr. Carr did not disguise his annoyance at the loss of his young disciple and firm ally. But an unlucky allusion to his previous remarks on Kearney's attentions to Jessie, and a querulous regret that he had permitted a disruption of their social intimacy, brought such an ominous and frigid opposition, not only from Christie, but even the frivolous Jessie herself, that Carr sank back in a crushed and terrified silence. "I only meant to say," he stammered after a pause, in which he, however, resumed his aggrieved manner, "that *Fairfax* seems to come here still, and *he* is not such a particular friend of mine."

"But he is — and has your interest entirely at heart," said Jessie, stoutly, "and he only comes here to tell us how things are going on at the works."

"And criticise your father, I suppose," said Mr. Carr, with an attempt at jocularity that did not, however, disguise an irritated suspiciousness. "He really seems to have supplanted *me* as he has poor Kearney in your estimation."

"Now, father," said Jessie, suddenly seizing him by the shoulders in affected indignation, but really to conceal a certain embarrassment that sprang quite as much from her sister's quietly observant eye as her father's speech, "you promised to let this ridiculous discussion drop. You will make me and Christie so nervous that we will not dare to open the door to a visitor, until he declares his innocence of any matrimonial intentions. You don't want to give color to the gossip that agreement with your views about the improvements is necessary to getting on with us."

"Who dares talk such rubbish?" said Carr, reddening; "is that the kind of gossip that Fairfax brings here?"

"Hardly, when it's known that he don't quite agree with you, and *does* come here. That's the best denial of the gossip."

Christie, who had of late loftily ignored

these discussions, waited until her father had taken his departure.

"Then that is the reason why you still see Mr. Munroe, after what you said," she remarked quietly to Jessie.

Jessie, who would have liked to escape with her father, was obliged to pause on the threshold of the door, with a pretty assumption of blank forgetfulness in her blue eyes and lifted eyebrows.

"Said what? when?" she asked vacantly.

"When — when Mr. Kearney that day — in the woods — went away," said Christie, faintly coloring.

"Oh! *that* day," said Jessie briskly; "the day he just gloved your hand with kisses, and then fled wildly into the forest to conceal his emotion."

"The day he behaved very foolishly," said Christie, with reproachful calmness, that did not, however, prevent a suspicion of indignant moisture in her eyes — " when you explained " —

"That it was n't meant for *me*," interrupted Jessie.

"That it was to you that *Mr. Munroe's* attentions were directed. And then we agreed that it was better to prevent any further advances of this kind by avoiding any familiar relations with either of them."

"Yes," said Jessie, "I remember; but you're not confounding my seeing Fairfax occasionally now with that sort of thing. *He* does n't kiss my hand like anything," she added, as if in abstract reflection.

"Nor run away, either," suggested the trodden worm, turning.

There was an ominous silence.

"Do you know we are nearly out of coffee?" said Jessie, choking, but moving towards the door with Spartan-like calmness.

"Yes. And something must be done this very day about the washing," said Christie, with suppressed emotion, going towards the opposite entrance.

Tears stood in each other's eyes with this terrible exchange of domestic confidences. Nevertheless, after a moment's pause, they deliberately turned again, and, facing each other with frightful calmness, left the room by purposeless and deliberate exits other than those they had contemplated — a crushing abnegation of self, that, to some extent, relieved their surcharged feelings.

Meantime the material prosperity of Devil's Ford increased, if a prosperity based upon no visible foundation but the confidence and hopes of its inhabitants could be called material. Few, if any, stopped to consider that the improvements, buildings, and business were simply the outlay of capital brought from elsewhere, and as yet the settlement or town, as it was now called, had neither produced nor exported capital of itself equal to half the amount expended. It was true that some land was cultivated on the further slope, some mills erected and lumber furnished from the inexhaustible forest; but the consumers were the inhabitants themselves, who paid for their produce in borrowed capital or unlimited credit. It was never discovered that while all roads led to Devil's Ford, Devil's Ford led to nowhere. The difficulties overcome in getting things into the settlement were never surmounted for getting things out of it. The lumber was practically valueless for export to other settlements across the mountain roads, which were equally rich in timber. The theory so enthusiastically held by the original locators, that Devil's Ford was a vast sink that had, through ages, exhausted and absorbed the trickling wealth of the adjacent hills and valleys, was suffering an ironical corroboration.

One morning it was known that work was stopped at the Devil's Ford Ditch — temporarily only, it was alleged, and many of the old workmen simply had their labor for the present transferred to excavating the river banks, and the collection of vast heaps of "pay gravel." Specimens from these mounds, taken from different localities, and at different levels, were sent to San Francisco for more rigid assay and analysis. It was believed that this would establish the fact of the permanent richness of the drifts, and not only justify past expenditure, but a renewed outlay of credit and capital. The suspension of engineering work gave Mr. Carr an opportunity to visit San Francisco on general business of the mine, which would not, however, prevent him from arranging further combinations with capital. His two daughters accompanied him. It offered an admirable opportunity for a shopping expedition, a change of scene, and a peaceful solution of their perplexing and anomalous social relations with Devil's Ford. In the first flush of gratitude to their father for this opportune holiday, something of harmony had been restored to the family circle that had of late been shaken by discord.

But their sanguine hopes of enjoyment were not entirely fulfilled. Both Jessie and Christie were obliged to confess to a certain disappointment in the aspect of the civilization they were now reëntering. They at first attributed it to the change in their own habits during the last three months, and their having become barbarous and countrified in their seclusion. Certainly in the matter of dress they were behind the fashions as revealed in Montgomery Street. But when the brief solace afforded them by the *modiste* and dressmaker was past, there seemed little else to be gained. They missed at first, I fear, the chivalrous and loyal devotion that had only amused them at Devil's Ford, and were the more inclined, I think, to distrust the conscious and more civilized gallantry of the better dressed and more carefully presented men they met. For it must be admitted that, for obvious reasons, their criticisms were at first confined to the sex they had been most in contact with. They could not help noticing that the men were more eager, annoyingly feverish, and self-asserting in their superior elegance and external show than their old associates were in their frank, unrestrained habits. It seemed to them that the five millionaires of Devil's Ford, in their radical simplicity and thoroughness, were perhaps nearer the type of true gentlemanhood than these citizens who imitated a civilization they were unable yet to reach.

The women simply frightened them, as being, even more than the men, demonstrative and excessive in their fine looks, their fine dresses, their extravagant demand for excitement. In less than a week they found themselves regretting — not the new villa on the slope of Devil's Ford, which even in its own *bizarre* fashion was exceeded by the barbarous ostentation of the villas and private houses around them — but the double cabin under the trees, which now seemed to them almost aristocratic in its grave simplicity and abstention. In the mysterious forest of masts that thronged the city's quays they recalled the straight shafts of the pines on Devil's slopes, only to miss the sedate repose and infinite calm that used to environ them. In the feverish, pulsating life of the young metropolis they often stopped oppressed, giddy, and choking; the roar of the streets and thoroughfares was meaningless to them, except to revive strange memories of the deep, unvarying monotone of the evening wind over their humbler roof on the Sierran hillside. Civic bred and nurtured as they were, the recurrence of these sensations perplexed and alarmed them.

"It seems so perfectly ridiculous," said Jessie, "for us to feel as out of place here as that Pike County servant girl in Sacramento who had never seen a steamboat before; do you know, I quite had a turn the other day at seeing a man on the Stockton wharf in a red shirt, with a rifle on his shoulder."

"And you wanted to go and speak to him?" said Christie, with a sad smile.

"No, that's just it; I felt awfully hurt and injured that he did not come up and speak to *me!* I wonder if we got any fever or that sort of thing up there; it makes one quite superstitious."

Christie did not reply; more than once before she had felt that inexplicable misgiving. It had sometimes seemed to her that she had never been quite herself since that memorable night when she had slipped out of their sleeping-cabin, and stood alone in the gracious and commanding presence of the woods and hills. In the solitude of night, with the hum of the great city rising below her — at times even in theatres or crowded assemblies of men and women — she forgot herself, and again stood in the weird brilliancy of that moonlight night in mute worship at the foot of that slowly-rising mystic altar of piled terraces, hanging forests, and lifted plateaus that climbed forever to the lonely skies. Again she felt before her the expanding and opening arms of the protecting woods. Had they really closed upon her in some pantheistic embrace that made her a part of them? Had she been baptized in that moonlight as a child of the great forest? It was easy to believe in the myths of the poets of an idyllic life under those trees, where, free from conventional restrictions, one loved and was loved. If she, with her own worldly experience, could think of this now, why might not George Kearney have thought? . . . She stopped, and found herself blushing even in the darkness. As the thought and blush were the usual sequel of her reflections, it is to be feared that they may have been at times the impelling cause.

Mr. Carr, however, made up for his

daughters' want of sympathy with metropolitan life. To their astonishment, he not only plunged into the fashionable gayeties and amusements of the town, but in dress and manner assumed the *rôle* of a leader of society. The invariable answer to their half-humorous comment was the necessities of the mine, and the policy of frequenting the company of capitalists, to enlist their support and confidence. There was something in this so unlike their father, that what at any other time they would have hailed as a relief to his habitual abstraction now half alarmed them. Yet he was not dissipated — he did not drink nor gamble. There certainly did not seem any harm in his frequenting the society of ladies, with a gallantry that appeared to be forced and a pleasure that to their critical eyes was certainly apocryphal. He did not drag his daughters into the mixed society of that period; he did not press upon them the company of those he most frequented, and whose accepted position in that little world of fashion was considered equal to their own.

When Jessie strongly objected to the pronounced manners of a certain widow, whose actual present wealth and pecuniary influence condoned for a more uncertain prehistoric past, Mr. Carr did not urge a further acquaintance. "As long as you're not thinking of marrying again, papa," Jessie had said finally, "I don't see the necessity of our knowing her." "But suppose I were," had replied Mr. Carr, with affected humor. "Then you certainly would n't care for any one like her," his daughter had responded triumphantly. Mr. Carr smiled, and dropped the subject, but it is probable that his daughters' want of sympathy with his acquaintances did not in the least interfere with his social prestige. A gentleman in all his relations and under all circumstances, even his cold scientific abstraction was provocative; rich men envied his lofty ignorance of the smaller details of money-making, even while they mistrusted his judgment. A man still well preserved, and free from weakening vices, he was a dangerous rival to younger and faster San Francisco, in the eyes of the sex, who knew how to value a repose they did not themselves possess.

Suddenly Mr. Carr announced his intention of proceeding to Sacramento, on further business of the mine, leaving his two daughters in the family of a wealthy friend until he should return for them. He opposed their ready suggestion to return to Devil's Ford with a new and unnecessary inflexibility: he even met their compromise to accompany him to Sacramento with equal decision.

"You will only be in my way," he said curtly. "Enjoy yourselves here while you can."

Thus left to themselves, they tried to accept his advice. Possibly some slight reaction to their previous disappointment may have already set in; perhaps they felt any distraction to be a relief to their anxiety about their father. They went out more; they frequented concerts and parties; they accepted, with their host and his family, an invitation to one of those opulent and barbaric entertainments with which a noted San

Francisco millionaire distracted his rare moments of reflection in his gorgeous palace on the hills. Here they would at least be once more in the country they loved, albeit of a milder and less heroic type, and a little degraded by the overlapping tinsel and scattered spangles of the palace.

It was a three days' *fête;* the style and choice of amusements left to the guests, and an equal and active participation by no means necessary or indispensable. Consequently, when Christie and Jessie Carr proposed a ride through the adjacent cañon on the second morning, they had no difficulty in finding horses in the well-furnished stables of their opulent entertainers, nor cavaliers among the other guests, who were too happy to find favor in the eyes of two pretty girls who were supposed to be abnormally fastidious and refined. Christie's escort was a good-natured young banker, shrewd enough to avoid demonstrative attentions, and lucky enough to interest her during the ride with his clear and half-humorous reflections on some of the business speculations of the day.

If his ideas were occasionally too clever, and not always consistent with a high sense of honor, she was none the less interested to know the ethics of that world of speculation into which her father had plunged, and the more convinced, with a mingled sense of pride and anxiety, that his still dominant gentlemanhood would prevent his coping with it on equal terms. Nor could she help contrasting the conversation of the sharp-witted man at her side with what she still remembered of the vague, touching, boyish enthusiasm of the millionaires of Devil's Ford. Had her escort guessed the result of this contrast, he would hardly have been as gratified as he was with the grave attention of her beautiful eyes.

The fascination of a gracious day and the leafy solitude of the cañon led them to prolong their ride beyond the proposed limit, and it became necessary towards sunset for them to seek some shorter cut home.

"There's a *vaquero* in yonder field," said Christie's escort, who was riding with her a little in advance of the others, "and those fellows know every trail that a horse can follow. I'll ride on, intercept him, and try my Spanish on him. If I miss him, as he's galloping on, you might try your hand on him yourself. He'll understand your eyes, Miss Carr, in any language."

As he dashed away, to cover his first audacity of compliment, Christie lifted the eyes thus apostrophized to the opposite field. The *vaquero*, who was chasing some cattle, was evidently too preoccupied to heed the shouts of her companion, and wheeling round suddenly to intercept one of the deviating fugitives, permitted Christie's escort to dash past him before that gentleman could rein in his excited steed. This brought the *vaquero* directly in her path. Perceiving her, he threw his horse back on its haunches, to prevent a collision. Christie rode up to him, suddenly uttered a cry, and halted. For before her, sunburnt in cheek and throat, darker in the free growth of moustache and curling hair, clad in the coarse, picturesque finery of his class, undisguised only in his boyish beauty, sat George Kearney.

The blood, that had forsaken her astonished face, rushed as quickly back. His eyes, which had suddenly sparkled with an electrical glow, sank before hers. His hand dropped, and his cheek flushed with a dark embarrassment.

"You here, Mr. Kearney? How strange! — but how glad I am to meet you again!"

She tried to smile; her voice trembled, and her little hand shook as she extended it to him.

He raised his dark eyes quickly, and impulsively urged his horse to her side. But, as if suddenly awakening to the reality of the situation, he glanced at her hurriedly, down at his barbaric finery, and threw a searching look towards her escort.

In an instant Christie saw the infelicity of her position, and its dangers. The words of Whiskey Dick, "He would n't stand that," flashed across her mind. There was no time to lose. The banker had already gained control over his horse, and was approaching them, all unconscious of the fixed stare with which George was regarding him.

Christie hastily seized the hand which he had allowed to fall at his side, and said quickly, —

"Will you ride with me a little way, Mr. Kearney?"

He turned the same searching look upon her. She met it clearly and steadily; he even thought reproachfully.

"Do!" she said hurriedly. "I ask it as a favor. I want to speak to you. Jessie and I are here alone. Father is away. *You* are one of our oldest friends."

He hesitated. She turned to the astonished young banker, who rode up.

"I have just met an old friend. Will you please ride back as quickly as you can, and tell Jessie that Mr. Kearney is here, and ask her to join us?"

She watched her dazed escort, still speechless from the spectacle of the fastidious Miss Carr *tête-à-tête* with a common Mexican *vaquero*, gallop off in the direction of the cañon, and then turned to George.

"Now take me home, the shortest way, as quick as you can."

"Home?" echoed George.

"I mean to Mr. Prince's house. Quick! before they can come up to us."

He mechanically put spurs to his horse; she followed. They presently struck into a trail that soon diverged again into a disused logging track through the woods.

"This is the short cut to Prince's, by two miles," he said, as they entered the woods.

As they were still galloping, without exchanging a word, Christie began to slacken her speed; George did the same. They were safe from intrusion at the present, even if the others had found the short cut. Christie, bold and self-reliant a moment ago, suddenly found herself growing weak and embarrassed. What had she done?

She checked her horse suddenly.

"Perhaps we had better wait for them," she said timidly.

George had not raised his eyes to hers.

"You said you wanted to hurry home," he replied gently, passing his hand along his mustang's velvety neck, "and — and you had something to say to me."

"Certainly," she answered, with a faint laugh. "I'm so astonished at meeting you here. I'm quite bewildered. You are living here; you have forsaken us to buy a ranche?" she continued, looking at him attentively.

His brow colored slightly.

"No, I'm living here, but I have bought no ranche. I'm only a hired man on somebody else's ranche, to look after the cattle."

He saw her beautiful eyes fill with astonishment and — something else. His brow cleared; he went on, with his old boyish laugh.

"No, Miss Carr. The fact is, I'm dead broke. I've lost everything since I saw you last. But as I know how to ride, and I'm not afraid of work, I manage to keep along."

"You have lost money in — in the mines?" said Christie suddenly.

"No" — he replied quickly, evading her eyes. "My brother has my interest, you know. I've been foolish on my own account solely. You know I'm rather inclined to that sort of thing. But as long as my folly don't affect others, I can stand it."

"But it may affect others — and *they* may not think of it as folly" — She stopped short, confused by his brightening color and eyes. "I mean — Oh, Mr. Kearney, I want you to be frank with me. I know nothing of business, but I know there has been trouble about the mine at Devil's Ford. Tell me honestly, has my father anything to do with it? If I thought that, through any imprudence of his, you had suffered — if I believed that you could trace any misfortune of yours to him — to *us* — I should never forgive myself " — she stopped and flashed a single look at him — " I should never forgive *you* for abandoning us."

The look of pain which had at first shown itself in his face, which never concealed anything, passed, and a quick smile followed her feminine anticlimax.

"Miss Carr," he said, with boyish eagerness, "if any man suggested to me that your father wasn't the brightest and best of his kind — too wise and clever for the fools about him to understand — I'd — I'd shoot him."

Confused by his ready and gracious disclaimer of what she had *not* intended to say, there was nothing left for her but to rush upon what she really intended to say, with what she felt was shameful precipitation.

"One word more, Mr. Kearney," she began, looking down, but feeling the color come to her face as she spoke. "When you spoke to me the day you left, you must have thought me hard and cruel. When I tell you that I thought you were alluding to Jessie and some feeling you had for her" —

"For Jessie!" echoed George.

"You will understand that — that" —

"That what?" said George, drawing nearer to her.

"That I was only speaking as she might have spoken had you talked to her of me," added Christie hurriedly, slightly backing her horse away from him.

But this was not so easy, as George was the better rider, and by an imperceptible movement of his wrist and foot had glued his horse to her side. "He will go now," she had thought, but he didn't.

"We must ride on," she suggested faintly.

"No," he said, with a sudden dropping of his boyish manner and a slight lifting of his head. "We must ride together no further, Miss Carr. I must go back to the work I am hired to do, and you must go on with your party, whom I hear coming. But when we part here you must bid me good-by — not as Jessie's sister — but as Christie — the one — the only woman that I love, or that I ever have loved."

He held out his hand. With the recollection of their previous parting, she tremblingly advanced her own. He took it, but did not raise it to his lips. And it was she who found herself half confusedly retaining his hand in hers, until she dropped it with a blush.

"Then is this the reason you give for deserting us as you have deserted Devil's Ford?" she said coldly.

He lifted his eyes to her with a strange smile, and said, "Yes," wheeled his horse, and disappeared in the forest.

He had left her thus abruptly once before, kissed, blushing, and indignant. He was leaving her now, unkissed, but white and indignant. Yet she was so self-possessed when the party joined her, that the singular rencontre and her explanation of the stranger's sudden departure excited no further comment. Only Jessie managed to whisper in her ear, —

"I hope you are satisfied now that it was n't me he meant?"

"Not at all," said Christie coldly.

CHAPTER VII.

A few days after the girls had returned to San Francisco, they received a letter from their father. His business, he wrote, would detain him in Sacramento some days longer. There was no reason why they should return to Devil's Ford in the heat of the summer; their host had written to beg him to allow them a more extended visit, and, if they were enjoying themselves, he thought it would be well not to disoblige an old friend. He had heard they had a pleasant visit to Mr. Prince's place, and that a certain young banker had been very attentive to Christie.

"Do you know what all this means, dear?" asked Jessie, who had been watching her sister with an unusually grave face.

Christie whose thoughts had wandered from the letter, replied carelessly, —

"I suppose it means that we are to wait here until father sends for us."

"It means a good deal more. It means that papa has had another reverse; it means that the assay has turned out badly for the mine — that the further they go from the flat the worse it gets — that all the gold they will probably ever see at Devil's Ford is what they have already found or will find on the flat; it means that all Devil's Ford is only a 'pocket,' and not a 'lead.'" She stopped, with unexpected tears in her eyes.

"Who told you this?" asked Christie breathlessly.

"Fairfax — Mr. Munroe," stammered her sister, "writes to me as if we already knew it — tells me not to be alarmed, that it is n't so bad — and all that."

"How long has this happened, Jessie?" said Christie, taking her hand, with a white but calm face.

"Nearly ever since we've been here, I suppose. It must be so, for he says poor papa is still hopeful of doing something yet."

"And Mr. Munroe writes to you?" said Christie abstractedly.

"Of course," said Jessie quickly. "He feels interested in — us."

"Nobody tells *me* anything," said Christie.

"Did n't " —

"No," said Christie bitterly.

"What on earth *did* you talk about? But people don't confide in you because they 're afraid of you. You 're so " —

"So what?"

"So gently patronizing, and so 'I-don't-suppose-you-can-help-it,-poor-thing,' in your general style," said Jessie, kissing her. "There! I only wish I was like you. What do you say if we write to father that we 'll go back to Devil's Ford? Mr. Munroe thinks we will be of service there just now. If the men are dissatisfied, and think we 're spending money " —

"I 'm afraid Mr. Munroe is hardly a disinterested adviser. At least, I don't think it would look quite decent for you to fly back without your father, at his suggestion," said Christie coldly. "He is not the only partner. We are spending no money. Besides, we have engaged to go to Mr. Prince's again next week."

"As you like, dear," said Jessie, turning away to hide a faint smile.

Nevertheless, when they returned from their visit to Mr. Prince's, and one or two uneventful rides, Christie looked grave. It was only a few days later that Jessie burst upon her one morning.

"You were saying that nobody ever tells you anything. Well, here's your chance. Whiskey Dick is below."

"Whiskey Dick?" repeated Christie. "What does he want?"

"*You*, love. Who else? You know he always scorns me as not being high-toned and elegant enough for his social confidences. He asked for you only."

With an uneasy sense of some impending revelation, Christie descended to the drawing-room. As she opened the door, a strong flavor of that toilet soap and eau de Cologne with which Whiskey Dick was in the habit of gracefully effacing the traces of dissipation made known his presence. In spite of a new suit of clothes, whose pristine folds refused to adapt themselves entirely to the contour of his figure, he was somewhat subdued by the unexpected elegance of the drawing-room of Christie's host. But a glance at Christie's sad, but gracious face quickly reassured him. Taking from his hat a three-cornered parcel, he unfolded a handsome *saffrona* rose, which he gravely presented to her. Having thus reëstablished his position, he sank elegantly into a *tête-à-tête* ottoman. Finding the position inconvenient to face Christie, who had seated herself on a chair, he transferred himself to the other side of the ottoman, and addressed her over its back as from a pulpit.

"Is this really a fortunate accident, Mr. Hall, or did you try to find us?" said Christie pleasantly.

"Partly promiskuss, and partly coincident, Miss Christie, one up and t' other down," said Dick lightly. "Work being slack at present at Devil's Ford, I reck'ned I'd take a *pasear* down to 'Frisco, and dip into the vortex o' fash'nable society and out again."

He lightly waved a new handkerchief to illustrate his swallow-like intrusion. "This yer minglin' with the *bo-tong* is apt to be wearisome, ez you and me knows, unless combined with experience and judgment. So when them boys up there allows that there's a little too much fash'nable society and San Francisco capital and high-falutin' about the future goin' on fer square surface mining, I sez, 'Look yere, gentlemen,' sez I, 'you don't see the pint. The pint is, to get the pop'lar eye fixed, so to speak, on Devil's Ford. When a fash'nable star rises above the 'Frisco horizon — like Miss Carr — and, so to speak, dazzles the gineral eye, people want to know who she is. And when people say that's the accomplished daughter o' the accomplished superintendent of the Devil's Ford claim — otherwise known as the Star-eyed Goddess o' Devil's Ford — every eye is fixed on the mine, and Capital, so to speak, tumbles to her.' And when they sez that the old man — excuse my freedom, but that's the way the boys talk of your father, meaning no harm — the old man, instead 'o trying to corral rich widders — grass or otherwise — to spend their money on the big works for the gold that ain't there yet — should stay in Devil's Ford and put all his *sabe* and genius into grindin' out the little gold that is there, I sez to them that it ain't your father's style. 'His style,' sez I, 'ez to go in and build them works.' When they're done he turns round to Capital, and sez he — 'Look, yer,' sez he, 'thar's all the works you want, first quality — cost a million; thar's all the water you want, onlimited — cost another million; thar's all the pay gravel you want in and outer the ground — call it two millions more. Now my time's too vally'ble; my professhun's too high-toned to *work* mines. I *make* 'em. Hand me over a check for ten millions and call it square, and work it for yourself.' So Capital hands over the money and waltzes down to run the mine, and you original locators walks round with yer hands in yer pockets a-top of your six million profit, and you let 's Capital take the work and the responsibility."

Preposterous as this seemed from the lips of Whiskey Dick, Christie had a haunting suspicion that it was not greatly unlike the theories expounded by the clever young banker who had been her escort. She did not interrupt his flow of reminiscent criticism; when he paused for breath, she said, quietly, —

"I met Mr. George Kearney the other day in the country."

Whiskey Dick stopped awkwardly, glanced hurriedly at Christie, and coughed behind his handkerchief.

"Mr. Kearney — eh — er — certengly — yes — er — met him, you say. Was he — er — er — well?"

"In health, yes; but otherwise he has lost everything," said Christie, fixing her eyes on the embarrassed Dick.

"Yes — er — in course — in course" — continued Dick, nervously glancing round the apartment as if endeavoring to find an opening to some less abrupt statement of the fact.

"And actually reduced to take some menial employment," added Christie, still regarding Dick with her clear glance.

"That's it — that's just it," said Dick, beaming as he suddenly found his delicate and confidential opportunity. "That's it, Miss Christie; that's just what I was sayin' to the boys. 'Ez it the square thing,' sez I, 'jest because George hez happened to hypothecate every dollar he has, or expects to hev, to put into them works, only to please Mr. Carr, and just because he don't want to distress that intelligent gentleman by letting him see he's dead broke — for him to go and demean himself and Devil's Ford by rushing away and hiring out as a Mexican *vaquero* on Mexican wages? Look,' sez I, 'at the disgrace he brings upon a high-toned, fash'nable girl, at whose side he's walked and danced, and passed rings, and sentiments, and bokays in the changes o' the cotillion and the mizzourka. And wot,' sez I, 'if some day, prancing along in a fash'nable cavalcade, she all of a suddents comes across him drivin' a Mexican steer?' That's what I said to the boys. And so you met him, Miss Christie, as usual," continued Dick, endeavoring under the appearance of a large social experience to conceal an eager anxiety to know the details — "so you met him; and, in course, you did n't let on yer knew him, so to speak, nat'rally, or p'raps you kinder like asked him to fix your saddle-girth, and give him a five dollar-piece — eh?"

Christie, who had risen and gone to the window, suddenly turned a very pale face and shining eyes on Dick.

"Mr. Hall," she said, with a faint attempt at a smile, "we are old friends, and I feel I can ask you a favor. You once before acted as our escort — it was for a short but a happy time — will you accept a larger trust? My father is busy in Sacramento for the mine: will you, without saying anything to anybody, take Jessie and me back at once to Devil's Ford?"

"Will I? Miss Christie," said Dick, choking between an intense gratification and a desire to keep back its vulgar exhibition, "I shall be proud!"

"When I say keep it a secret" — she hesitated — "I don't mean that I object to your letting Mr. Kearney, if you happen to know where he is, understand that we are going back to Devil's Ford."

"Cert'nly — nat'rally," said Dick, waving his hand gracefully; "sorter drop him a line, saying that bizness of a social and delicate nature — being the escort of Miss Christie and Jessie Carr to Devil's Ford — prevents my having the pleasure of calling."

"That will do very well, Mr. Hall," said Christie, faintly smiling through her moist eyelashes. "Then will you go at once and secure tickets for to-night's boat, and bring them here? Jessie and I will arrange everything else."

"Cert'nly," said Dick impulsively, and preparing to take a graceful leave.

"We'll be impatient until you return with the tickets," said Christie graciously.

Dick shook hands gravely, got as far as the door, and paused.

"You think it better to take the tickets now?" he said dubiously.

"By all means," said Christie impetuously. "I've set my heart on going to-night — and unless you secure berths early" —

"In course — in course," interrupted Dick nervously. "But" —

"But what?" said Christie impatiently.

Dick hesitated, shut the door carefully, and, looking round the room, lightly shook out his handkerchief, apparently flicked away an embarrassing suggestion, and said, with a little laugh, —

"It's ridiklous, perfectly ridiklous, Miss Christie; but not bein' in the habit of carryin' ready money, and havin' omitted to cash a draft on Wells, Fargo & Co." —

"Of course," said Christie rapidly. "How forgetful I am! Pray forgive me, Mr. Hall. I did n't think. I'll run up and get it from our host; he will be glad to be our banker."

"One moment, Miss Christie," said Dick lightly, as his thumb and finger relaxed in his waistcoat pocket over the only piece of money in the world that had remained to him after his extravagant purchase of Christie's *saffrona* rose, "one moment: in this yer monetary transaction, if you like, you are at liberty to use *my* name."

CHAPTER VIII.

As Christie and Jessie Carr looked from the windows of the coach, whose dust-clogged wheels were slowly dragging them, as if reluctant, nearer the last stage of their journey to Devil's Ford, they were conscious of a change in the landscape, which they could not entirely charge upon their changed feelings. The few bared open spaces on the upland, the long stretch of rocky ridge near the summit, so vivid and so velvety during their first journey, were now burnt and yellow; even the brief openings in the forest were seared as if by a hot iron in the scorching rays of a half year's sun. The pastoral slopes of the valley below were cloaked in lustreless leather: the rare watercourses along the road had faded from the waiting eye and ear; it seemed as if the long and dry summer had even invaded the close-set ranks of pines, and had blown a simoom breath through the densest woods, leaving its charred red ashes on every leaf and spray along the tunnelled shade. As they leaned out of the window and inhaled the half-dead spices of the evergreens, they seemed to have entered the atmosphere of some exhausted passion — of some fierce excitement that was even now slowly burning itself out.

It was a relief at last to see the straggling houses of Devil's Ford far below come once more into view, as they rounded the shoulder of Devil's Spur and began the long descent. But as they entered the town a change more ominous and startling than the desiccation of the landscape forced itself upon them. The town was still there, but where were the inhabitants? Four months ago they had left the straggling street thronged with busy citizens — groups at every corner, and a chaos of merchandise and traders in the open *plaza* or square beside the Presbyterian church. Now all was changed. Only a few wayfarers lifted their heads lazily as the coach rattled by, crossing the deserted square littered with empty boxes, and gliding past empty cabins or vacant shop windows, from which not only familiar faces, but even the window sashes themselves, were gone. The great unfinished serpent-like flume, crossing the river on gigantic trestles, had advanced as far as the town, stooping over it like some enormous reptile that had sucked its life blood and was gorged with its prey.

Whiskey Dick, who had left the stage on the summit to avail himself of a shorter foot trail to the house, that would give him half an hour's grace to make preparations, met them at the stage office with a buggy. A glance at the young girls, perhaps, convinced him that the graces of elegant worldly conversation were out of place with the revelation he read on their faces. Perhaps he, too, was a trifle indisposed. The short journey to the house was made in profound silence.

The villa had been repainted and decorated, and it looked fresher, and even, to their preoccupied minds, appeared more attractive than ever. Thoughtful hands had taken care of the vines and rose-bushes on the trellises; water — that precious element in Devil's Ford — had not been spared in keeping green through the long drought the plants which the girls had so tenderly nurtured. It was the one oasis in which the summer still lingered; and yet a singular sense of loss came over the girls as they once more crossed its threshold. It seemed no longer their own.

"Ef I was you, Miss Christie, I'd keep close to the house for a day or two, until — until — things is settled," said Dick; "there's a heap o' tramps and sich cattle trapsin' round. P'raps you would n't feel so lonesome if you was nearer town — for instance, 'bout wher' you useter live."

"In the dear old cabin," said Christie quickly; "I remember it; I wish we were there now."

"Do you really? Do you?" said Whiskey Dick, with suddenly twinkling eyes. "That's like you to say it. That's what I allus said," continued Dick, addressing space generally; "if there's any one ez knows how to come square down to the bottom rock without flinchin', it's your high-toned, fash'nable gals. But I must meander back to town, and let the boys know you're in possession, safe and sound. It's right mean that Fairfax and Mattingly had to go down to Lagrange on some low business yesterday, but they'll be back to-morrow. So long."

Left alone, the girls began to realize their strange position. They had conceived no settled plan. The night they left San Francisco they had written an earnest letter to their father, telling him that on learning the truth about the reverses of Devil's Ford, they thought it their duty to return and share them with others, without obliging him to prefer the request, and with as little worry to him as possible. He would find them ready to share his trials, and in what must be the scene of their work hereafter.

"It will bring father back," said Christie; "he won't leave us here alone; and then together we must come to some understanding with him — with *them* — for somehow I feel as if this house belonged to us no longer."

Her surmise was not far wrong. When Mr. Carr arrived hurriedly from Sacramento the next evening, he found the house deserted. His daughters were gone; there were indications that they had arrived, and, for some reason, suddenly departed. The vague fear that had haunted his guilty soul after receiving their letter, and during his breathless journey, now seemed to be realized. He was turning from the empty house, whose reproachful solitude frightened him, when he was confronted on the threshold by the figure of Fairfax Munroe.

"I came to the stage office to meet you," he said; "you must have left the stage at the summit."

"I did," said Carr angrily. "I was anxious to meet my daughters quickly, to know the reason of their foolish alarm, and to know also who had been frightening them. Where are they?"

"They are safe in the old cabin beyond, that has been put up ready to receive them again," said Fairfax quietly.

"But what is the meaning of this? Why

are they not here?" demanded Carr, hiding his agitation in a burst of querulous rage.

"Do *you* ask, Mr. Carr?" said Fairfax sadly. "Did you expect them to remain here until the sheriff took possession? No one knows better than yourself that the money advanced you on the deeds of this homestead has never been repaid."

Carr staggered, but recovered himself with feeble violence.

"Since you know so much of my affairs, how do you know that this claim will ever be pressed for payment? How do you know it is not the advance of a — a — friend?"

"Because I have seen the woman who advanced it," said Fairfax hopelessly. "She was here to look at the property before your daughters came."

"Well?" said Carr nervously.

"Well! You force me to tell you something I should like to forget. You force me to anticipate a disclosure I expected to make to you only when I came to ask permission to woo your daughter Jessie; and when I tell you what it is, you will understand that

I have no right to criticise your conduct. I am only explaining my own."

"Go on," said Carr impatiently.

"When I first came to this country, there was a woman I loved passionately. She treated me as women of her kind only treat men like me, she ruined me, and left me. That was four years ago. I love your daughter, Mr. Carr, but she has never heard it from my lips. I would not woo her until I had told you all. I have tried to do it ere this, and failed. Perhaps I should not now, but " —

"But what?" said Carr furiously; "speak out!"

"But this. Look!" said Fairfax, producing from his pocket the packet of letters Jessie had found; "perhaps you know the handwriting?"

"What do you mean?" gasped Carr.

"That woman — my mistress — is the woman who advanced you money, and who claims this house."

. . . .

The interview, and whatever came of it,

remained a secret with the two men. When Mr. Carr accepted the hospitality of the old cabin again, it was understood that he had sacrificed the new house and its furniture to some of the more pressing debts of the mine, and the act went far to restore his waning popularity. But a more genuine feeling of relief was experienced by Devil's Ford when it was rumored that Fairfax Munroe had asked for the hand of Jessie Carr, and that some promise, contingent upon the equitable adjustment of the affairs of the mine, had been given by Mr. Carr. To the superstitious mind of Devil's Ford and its few remaining locators, this new partnership seemed to promise that unity of interest and stability of fortune that Devil's Ford had lacked. But nothing could be done until the rainy season had set fairly in; until the long-looked-for element that was to magically separate the gold from the dross in those dull mounds of dust and gravel had come of its own free will, and in its own appointed channels, independent of the feeble auxiliaries that had hopelessly riven the rocks on the hillside, or hung incomplete and unfinished in lofty scaffoldings above the settlement.

The rainy season came early. At first in gathered mists on the higher peaks that were lifted in the morning sun only to show a fresher field of dazzling white below; in white clouds that at first seemed to be mere drifts blown across from those fresh snow-fields, and obscuring the clear blue above; in far-off murmurs in the hollow hills and gulches; in nearer tinkling melody and baby prattling in the leaves. It came with bright flashes of sunlight by day, with deep, monotonous shadow at night; with the onset of heavy winds, the roar of turbulent woods, the tumultuous tossing of leafy arms, and with what seemed the silent dissolution of the whole landscape in days of steady and uninterrupted downfall. It came extravagantly, for every cañon had grown into a torrent, every gulch a waterspout, every watercourse a river, and all pouring into the North Fork, that, rushing past the settlement, seemed to threaten it with lifted crest and flying mane. It came dangerously, for one night the river, leaping the feeble barrier of Devil's Ford, swept away houses and banks, scattered with unconscious irony the laboriously collected heaps of gravel left for hydraulic machinery, and spread out a vast and silent lake across the submerged flat.

In the hurry and confusion of that night, the girls had thrown open their cabin to the escaping miners, who hurried along the slope that was now the bank of the river. Suddenly Christie felt her arm grasped, and she was half led, half dragged, into the inner room. Her father stood before her.

" Where is George Kearney ? " he asked tremulously.

" George Kearney ! " echoed Christie, for a moment believing the excitement had turned her father's brain. " You know he is not here ; he is in San Francisco."

" He is here — I tell you," said Carr impatiently ; " he has been here ever since the high water, trying to save the flume and reservoir."

" George — here ! " Christie could only gasp.

"Yes! He passed here a few moments ago, to see if you were all safe, and he has gone on towards the flume. But what he is trying to do is madness. If you see him, implore him to do no more. Let him abandon the accursed flume to its fate. It has worked already too much woe upon us all; why should it carry his brave and youthful soul down with it?"

The words were still ringing in her ears, when he suddenly passed away, with the hurrying crowd. Scarcely knowing what she did, she ran out, vaguely intent only on one thought, seeking only the one face, lately so dear in recollection that she felt she would die if she never saw it again. Perplexed by confused voices in the woods, she lost track of the crowd, until the voices suddenly were raised in one loud outcry, followed by the crashing of timber, the splashing of water, a silence, and then a dull, continuous roar. She ran vaguely on in the direction of the reservoir, with her father's injunction still in her mind, until a terrible idea displaced it, and she turned at right angles suddenly, and ran towards the slope leading down to the submerged flat. She had barely left the shelter of the trees behind her before the roar of water seemed to rise at her very feet. She stopped, dazed, bewildered, and horror-stricken, on the edge of the slope. It was the slope no longer, but the bank of the river itself!

Even in the gray light of early morning, and with inexperienced eyes, she saw all too clearly now. The trestle-work had given way; the curving mile of flume, fallen into the stream, and crushed and dammed against the opposite shore, had absolutely turned the whole river through the half-finished ditch and partly excavated mine in its way, a few rods further on to join the old familiar channel. The bank of the river was changed; the flat had become an island, between which and the slope where she stood the North Fork was rolling its resistless yellow torrent. As she gazed spellbound, a portion of the slope beneath her suddenly seemed to sink and crumble, and was swallowed up in the rushing stream. She heard a cry of warning behind her, but, rooted to the spot by a fearful fascination, she heeded it not. Again there was a sudden disruption, and another part of the slope sank to rise no more; but this time she felt herself seized by the waist and dragged back. It was her father standing by her side.

He was flushed and excited, gazing at the water with a strange exultation.

"Do you see it? Do you know what has happened?" he asked quickly.

"The flume has fallen and turned the river," said Christie hurriedly. "But — have you seen him — is he safe?"

"He — who?" he answered vacantly.

"George Kearney!"

"He is safe," he said impatiently. "But, do you see, Christie? Do you know what this means?"

He pointed with his tremulous hand to the stream before them.

"It means we are ruined," said Christie coldly.

"Nothing of the kind! It means that the river is doing the work of the flume. It is sluicing off the gravel, deepening the ditch, and altering the slope which was the old bend of the river. It will do in ten minutes the work that would take us a year. If we can stop it in time, or control it, we are safe; but if we cannot, it will carry away the bed and deposit with the rest, and we are ruined again."

With a gesture of impotent fury, he dashed away in the direction of an equally excited crowd, that on a point of the slope nearer the island were gesticulating and shouting to a second group of men, who on the opposite shore were clambering on over the choked *débris* of the flume that had dammed and diverted the current. It was evident that the same idea had occurred to them, and they were risking their lives in the attempt to set free the impediments. Shocked and indignant as Christie had been at the degrading absorption of material interests at such a moment, the element of danger lifted the labors of these men into heroism, and she began to feel a strange exultation as she watched them. Under the skilful blows of their axes, in a few moments the vast body of drift began to disintegrate, and then to swing round and move towards the old channel. A cheer went up, but as suddenly died away again. An overlapping fringe of wreckage had caught on the point of the island and arrested the whole mass.

The men, who had gained the shore with difficulty, looked back with a cry of despair. But the next moment from among them leaped a figure, alert, buoyant, invincible, and, axe in hand, once more essayed the passage. Springing from timber to timber he at last reached the point of obstruction. A few strokes of the axe were sufficient to clear it; but at the first stroke it was apparent that the striker was also losing his hold upon the shore, and that he must inevitably be carried away with the tossing *débris*. But this consideration did not seem to affect him; the last blow was struck, and as the freed timbers rolled on, over and over, he boldly plunged into the flood. Christie gave a little cry — her heart had bounded with him; it seemed as if his plunge had splashed the water in her eyes. He did not come to the surface until he had passed the point below where her father stood, and then struggling feebly, as if stunned or disabled by a blow. It seemed to her that he was trying to approach the side of the river where she was. Would he do it? Could she help him? She was alone; he was hidden from the view of the men on the point, and no succor could come from them. There was a fringe of alder nearly opposite their cabin that almost overhung the stream. She ran to it, clutched it with a frantic hand, and, leaning over the boiling water, uttered for the first time his name.

"George!"

As if called to the surface by the magic of her voice, he rose a few yards from her in mid-current, and turned his fading eyes towards the bank. In another moment he would have been swept beyond her reach, but with a supreme effort he turned on one side; the current, striking him sideways, threw him towards the bank, and she caught him by his sleeve. For an instant it seemed as if she would be dragged down with him. For one dangerous moment she did not care, and almost yielded to the spell; but as the rush of water pressed him against the bank, she recovered herself, and managed to lift him beyond its reach. And then she sat down, half fainting, with his white face and damp curls upon her breast.

"George, darling, speak to me! Only one word! Tell me, have I saved you?"

His eyes opened. A faint twinkle of the old days came to them — a boyish smile played upon his lips.

"For yourself — or Jessie?"

She looked around her with a little frightened air. They were alone. There was but one way of sealing those mischievous lips, and she found it!

. . . .

"That's what I allus said, gentlemen," lazily remarked Whiskey Dick, a few weeks later, leaning back against the bar, with his glass in his hand. "'George,' sez I, 'it ain't what you *say* to a fash'nable, high-toned young lady; it's what you *does* ez makes or breaks you.' And that's what I sez gin'rally o' things in the Ford. It ain't what Carr and you boys allows to do; it's the gin'ral average o' things ez *iz* done that gives tone to the hull, and hez brought this yer new luck to you all!"

317 pages

www.ingramcontent.com/pod-product-compliance
Lightning Source LLC
Chambersburg PA
CBHW030744230426
43667CB00007B/835